D0555464

THE WHITE PAGE

An Bhileog Bhán

Twentieth-Century Irish Women Poets

Edited by
Joan McBreen

for Christine,

*" I put my lips to the water
and came so gently
into love's sanctuary."*

(p. 201)

from Joan McBreen

7/12/99, Tuam, G. Galway

Salmon Publishing

Published in 1999 by
Salmon Publishing Ltd.,
Cliffs of Moher, County Clare, Ireland
http://www.salmonpoetry.com
email: salpub@iol.ie

© Joan McBreen 1999
The moral right of the author has been asserted.

A catalogue record for this book is available from the British Library.

The Arts Council
An Chomhairle Ealaíon

Salmon Publishing gratefully acknowledges
the financial assistance of The Arts Council.

ISBN 1 897648 57 X Paperback
ISBN 1 897648 40 5 Hardback

All rights reserved. No part of this publication may be reproduced or transmitted in
any form or by any means, electronic or mechanical, including photography,
recording, or any information storage or retrieval system, without permission in
writing from the publisher. The book is sold subject to the condition that it shall
not, by way of trade or otherwise, be lent, resold or otherwise circulated without
the publisher's prior consent in any form of binding or cover other than that in
which it is published and without a similar condition, including this condition,
being imposed on the subsequent purchaser.

The title of this book, *The White Page / An Bhileog Bhán* is taken from a poem of
the same name by Caitlín Maude. From *Caitlín Maude, Dánta*, Ciarán Ó Coigligh a
chuir in eagar. Baile Átha Cliath, Coiscéim (1984), and from *Caitlín Maude: file,
poet, poeta*. Italy, edizioni dal sud (1985). By kind permission of Cathal Ó Luain.

Cover painting from *Uaimh Series*, 1996. Mixed media on canvas.
By kind permission of Gwen O'Dowd.

Printed by Techman Ireland Ltd., Dublin

By the same author

POETRY

The Wind Beyond the Wall. (1990, 1991). Oregon, Story Line Press.
A Walled Garden in Moylough. (1995). Oregon, Story Line Press / County Galway, Salmon Publishing.

This book is a comprehensive study of Irish women's poetry published in book form in the twentieth century. It is an extended annotated directory, with biographical and bibliographical details on each poet. Poems and photographs, generously donated by the poets themselves, are also included. Poets born in the Republic of Ireland and Northern Ireland, as well as poets of Irish ancestry and non-nationals resident and writing in Ireland for long periods, are represented. A reference book for students of Irish literature, it is also a poetry anthology featuring more than 100 poets who have published at least one collection.

Joan McBreen is from Sligo; she now lives in Tuam, County Galway. Her poetry collections are *The Wind Beyond the Wall* (Story Line Press, Oregon, 1990; reprinted 1991) and *A Walled Garden in Moylough* (Story Line Press and Salmon Publishing, County Galway, 1995). She trained and worked as a primary teacher for many years. In 1997 she was awarded an MA degree in Women's Studies by University College, Dublin, presenting *A Dictionary of Twentieth-Century Irish Women Poets* as her dissertation. Her poetry is published widely in Ireland and abroad and has been broadcast, anthologised and translated into many languages.

STUDYING THE LANGUAGE

On Sundays I watch the hermits coming out of their holes
Into the light. Their cliff is as full as a hive.
They crowd together on warm shoulders of rock
Where the sun has been shining, their joints crackle.
They begin to talk after a while.
I listen to their accents, they are not all
From this island, not all old,
Not even, I think, all masculine.

They are so wise, they do not pretend to see me.
They drink from the scattered pools of melted snow:
I walk right by them and drink when they have done.
I can see the marks of chains around their feet.

I call this my work, these decades and stations –
Because, without these, I would be a stranger here.

Eiléan Ní Chuilleanáin

This book is dedicated
to the memory of
Anne Kennedy
1935 – 1998

Contents

Guest Introductions

As Minister for Arts, Heritage, Gaeltacht and the Islands I am delighted to be afforded the opportunity to lend my support to Joan McBreen and Salmon Publishing on the publication of *The White Page / An Bhileog Bhán – Twentieth-Century Irish Women Poets*.

The work that Joan McBreen has done in bringing this to fruition has given recognition to the importance and central role of women in the history of Irish literature. As well as being an anthology of poetry it also stands as a reference book for students of literature and the women's movement. I believe it makes an enormous contribution in acknowledging the role of women poets in Irish history.

I would like to take this opportunity to congratulate Joan and all those who assisted and supported her in preparing *The White Page / An Bhileog Bhán*. I wish her every success with this publication. I am sure the drive, dedication and enthusiasm she has displayed will lead to us enjoying future publications.

Síle de Valera T.D.
Minister for Arts, Heritage, Gaeltacht and the Islands
Dáil Éireann, 2nd September 1999

Working as a Radio Producer with RTÉ over the past fifteen years, mainly in the area of arts, literature and documentary programmes, I have been struck very strongly by the emergence of the clear and unequivocal voices of Irish women poets. Indeed these voices of Irish women, demanding and deserving to be heard, have enlivened writers' workshops, poetry platforms and countless publications at home and abroad. It is as if the voices of Irish women are at last being heard after a thousand years of silence.

In this context, the publication of *The White Page / An Bhileog Bhán*, edited by Joan McBreen and published by the ever-enterprising Salmon Publishing is, for many reasons, a timely landmark in Irish publishing. It is primarily a comprehensive study of poetry published by Irish women in book form in the twentieth century. This important and long overdue addition to the canon of Irish writing is a scholarly yet accessible introduction, directory, exposition and celebration of the work of over one hundred published Irish women poets, many of whom have been unjustly overlooked or ignored in the real and vital contribution they have made to the story of our century.

By her own inclusive terms of reference Joan McBreen , in this anthology, has cast her nets wide, including in her definition of Irish women poets writers born in Northern Ireland as well as in the Republic alongside poets of Irish ancestry and non-nationals resident and writing in the country.

This anthology proves beyond any doubt that by ignoring or not taking seriously the significant contribution to Irish literature made over the years by our women poets we are experiencing only half the story. Irish women poets may justly feel aggrieved by this exclusion but it is all of us, male and female, who are truly deprived and diminished by the loss.

Here is a rich treasure house of hidden gold, a host of lost voices deserving to be heard and an amazing and rich addition to the understanding and celebration of who and what we are that will find recognition and resonance in every human heart.

Seamus Hosey
Senior Producer, RTÉ Radio
October 1999

She is holding out her hand
to catch a thread which is stretching
around a corner.

She is offered nothing back. There is a labyrinth
she must enter over there.

Joan McBreen

Can it really be so long ago, that quicksilver flash of time?

I started looking for poems by Irish women, thirty years ago
or thereabouts, a young woman desperate to see in a culture
whose unyielding surfaces seemed to offer no reflections of living
and imagining to illuminate my own (scant) experience and desire.
It was, to be sure, a ruthlessly selfish search. I wanted to breathe.
I wanted to know other possibilities. I wanted poems I could live by.
Like other women of my generation and background – middle class,
urban, educated, privileged woman that I was, still am – eventually,
slowly, learning to look in nooks and crannies, always on the *qui
vive*, I found them here and there, those precious poems by women
who opened up new possibilities of being and becoming.

But that was another era, almost another country. In that flash
of time, so much has been revealed and re-imagined. Women
writers, artists, scholars, readers, thinkers, activists have entered
the labyrinth and caught the thread of our complicated breathing
and living, holding it fast, offering it to all seekers of the depths
below the harsh surfaces.

The White Page / An Bhileog Bhán is no trick of history or
accident of fate. A work of scholarship in the very finest sense –
careful, timely, intelligent and imaginative – it is above all a work of
love by a remarkable woman living through times of great challenge,
bravely risking the labyrinth and generously offering us all that she
finds there. Thank you, Joan.

Ailbhe Smyth
Director,
Women's Education Research and Resource Centre (WERRC)
University College, Dublin
September 18th, 1999

Editor's Introduction

Some of what we love
we stumble upon –
a purse of gold thrown on the road,
a poem, a friend, a great song.

Moya Cannon

In 1994, Anne Ulry Colman was compiling a dictionary of women poets: poets who wrote in English, had been born in Ireland between 1800 and 1899, and whose work was published before 1931. When asked by Colman to name as many nineteenth-century poets as I could, I named six. In her completed volume *A Dictionary of Nineteenth-Century Irish Women Poets* (1996) Colman identified more than three hundred Irish women writing poetry during that period. Among these were women who had also published volumes of prose, were hymnists and translators of poetry, or had published single poems or sequences of poems in newspapers and magazines. Thus she dispelled one of the gender-related myths, that there were few, if any, Irish women poets writing in the nineteenth and early twentieth centuries.

A seed had been sown in my mind. I began to compile a list of twentieth-century Irish women poets only to discover that many poets published during this period were already suffering neglect and even invisibility. The result is this book which records and celebrates Irish women's voices in twentieth-century poetry, published in volume form. The poets included here are, with few exceptions, born after 1920. They are Irish by birth, descent or adoption, and they identify themselves or their work with Ireland.

The literary myth that there was little interest in women's writing prior to the mid-twentieth-century in Ireland, is being contradicted by current academic scholarship in the field. The growth of interest in Irish Studies in universities and colleges throughout the United States is serving to alter the map of poetry for women no less than for men. The claim that women writers, poets in particular, were isolated in their endeavours is also a myth. Many women poets of the late nineteenth and early twentieth centuries were linked to more powerful and publicly acknowledged male poets. They enjoyed literary success during their lifetimes; publishing houses published their work and the literary establishment was not prejudiced against them. An examination of themes used demonstrates that those of domestic life and motherhood occurred frequently in the poetry of these women. The exploration and rediscovery of Irish culture and identity during the Irish Literary Revival, together with a growing feminist consciousness, suggests there was a vigorous atmosphere surrounding their work. W.B. Yeats' belief, for example, in the value of female experience as a subject for poetry was astute and sincere. His close friend and fellow poet, Katherine Tynan, among others, was praised and encouraged by him.

Dr. Colman's work demonstrated that women published verse abundantly during a supposedly dark period. She clearly pointed to the 1930s as the start of the real dark ages. Some reasons for this include censorship, conservative Catholicism, few Irish publishing houses, the decline of the Anglo-Irish, the post-Civil War period, the outbreak of the Second World War and the uncertainties, aesthetic and economic, that plagued mid-twentieth-century Ireland. Lack of educational opportunities, poverty and a traditional culture which defined women as home-makers, wives and mothers exclusively, are also significant factors.

The women's movement began in earnest in Ireland in 1970. Much change has affected the social, cultural and educational climate, in particular for Ireland's women, since the mid-twentieth century. Issues addressed by feminism are issues that have been addressed by feminism everywhere in the world, the most crucial being political, sexual and cultural freedoms and the granting of personal identity. In his introduction to *Irish Poetry Since Kavanagh* (1996), Theo Dorgan wrote:

> It seems clear by now that the gender battles will be carried to a successful conclusion – any genuinely attentive reader of contemporary Irish poetry knows that the standard-bearers for the next century will be found equally among the women poets as among the men now coming into their stride. We have been enormously disadvantaged by the psychic wound which has deprived us in our poetry until now of the autonomous voices of women. Given that the price of freedom is eternal vigilance, I predict we will be liberated into a poetry written as much by vigilant women as by men. I do not think the implications of this have yet been fully recognised. It is not so much that, using essence in the Aristotelian sense, women have a voice essentially different from men. It is more useful to think of it as the coming into written discourse of half the human population. We are richer in human resource than we had ever guessed.

Dorgan was aware that the silence which surrounded the voices of women in poetry throughout the decades after 1930 was being broken and that it was necessary for all poets and thinkers to recognise and begin to celebrate this change. That this recognition and celebration were, however, slow to appear deserves attention.

Anthologies represent current talents and tastes in the poetry of any culture. In many anthologies published throughout the last few decades there was a serious under-representation of poetry written by women. Contemporary poets, such as Eiléan Ní Chuilleanáin, Eavan Boland, Eithne Strong and Máire Mac an tSaoi, who by 1980 had published substantial bodies of work, were omitted from the *New Oxford Book of Irish Verse*, edited by Thomas Kinsella in 1986. *The Penguin Book of Irish Verse*, edited by Brendan Kennelly in 1970, includes only five women. Patrick Crotty's 1995 volume, *Modern Irish Poetry – an Anthology*, includes seven women. *Contemporary Irish Poetry*, the 1990 anthology edited by Peter Fallon and Derek Mahon, includes four women and Sebastian Barry's 1986 volume, *The Inherited Boundaries – Younger Poets of the Republic of Ireland*, excludes women entirely. More recently, *The Field Day Anthology of Irish Literature* was published in 1991, under the general editorship of Seamus Deane. Its inclusion of only four women poets with thirty-seven male poets by its all male editorial board raised many important and interesting questions.

Three anthologies, published since 1950, attempted to introduce balance to the representation and development of women's poetic voices in this century. In 1958, in his introduction to the *Oxford Book of Irish Verse*, Donagh MacDonagh (who, with his co-editor Lennox Robinson, included seventeen women in his volume) also defined the Irish poet by birth, descent or adoption. *Pillars of the House – an Anthology of Verse by Irish Women from 1690 to the Present* (Kelly,1988) was the first anthology of Irish women's poetry to chronologically follow the development of such poetry and included over one hundred and forty poems from eighty women writers. Ailbhe Smyth's *Wildish Things – an Anthology of New Irish Women's Writing* was published in 1989. These anthologies are testimonies to the range and diversity of the lives and vision of women writing both in prose and poetry in contemporary Ireland. In 1985 Ruth Hooley edited *The Female Line*, a collection of writings by Northern Irish women. Its focus was a breakthrough for all women writers North and South of the border.

This book details the work of more than one hundred Irish women poets. Only a handful are known to the world at large. Awareness of this raises the question of who gets in and who stays out of the canon and why. The poetry market is small, readership a minority, no less in Ireland than elsewhere. The few Irish women poets who have been taken up by British and American publishers are more likely to make it into the canon. Irish writers have traditionally looked to Britain for publication; poets are no exception. Faber and Faber, Carcanet, Bloodaxe and others publish many of our best known contemporary poets, most of whom, until recent years, have been men. Also, traditionally, women have been figures or icons in Irish poems rather than poets themselves. A real sea-change began in the 1970s and has gained ground steadily since then. Prior to this, isolated volumes of poetry by women appeared from the Dolmen Press such as Máire Mhac an tSaoi's *A Heart Full of Thought: Translations from Classical Gaelic Poetry* in 1959, Juanita Casey's *Horse by the River and other poems* in 1968, Anne Cluysenaar's *Nodes: Selected Poems* in 1971. Leland Bardwell's *The Mad Cyclist* was published by New Writer's Press in 1970. The Gallery Press, founded in 1970, published Eiléan Ní Chuilleanáin's first collection *Acts and Monuments* in 1972. In 1975 Arlen House was founded and published contemporary writing, though not primarily poetry, by women. However, four volumes of Eavan Boland's poetry appeared from this press in the 1980s. This was followed by the feminist press Attic, founded in 1983. Others such as Raven Arts Press, Beaver Row Press, Dedalus Press, Blackstaff Press, Cló Iar Chonnachta, Coiscéim and Salmon Publishing emerged as publishing houses throughout the 1980s. While all these presses published the work of some women poets few represented male and female work evenly. Salmon Publishing has been the most receptive and consistent.

Much has been said and written on the subject of Irish women writers and gender questions in general since 1970. International feminism has had an influence on poetry together with influencing other struggles women in Ireland have experienced. While woman and poet, woman writer and silence, woman, sacrifice and creativity, poetry and feminism, and woman and Ireland, remain key notes of debate there are other notes that merit attention. Problems in relation to reviewing, literary criticism, influence, support, economic and otherwise, remain part of the ongoing cultural debate or discourse.

As is evident from the biographical annotations in this book, the workshop is important to many women poets. In the 1980s Eavan Boland, arguably more than any other established poet, made a feminist commitment to help emerging women poets, leading workshops in Dublin and elsewhere in the country. From her position now at Stanford University in the USA she promotes the work of Irish women poets and is in touch with the publishing changes that have taken place as we enter the twenty-first century.

The situation in 1999, with regard to women and writing poetry in Ireland, is thankfully happier than it was in the 1950s and 1960s. As I worked on this book, I became aware of a deep sense of a self-confident female poet emerging, ready to explore female identity and to challenge the previously received images of women in Irish history, culture and literature. Women are now more visible in workshops and in community writing groups, indicating a further confidence in the value of their poetry and their publishing prospects. At local, national and international levels, they are taking their share of literary prizes, bursaries and travel grants. I believe the state of Irish women's poetry to be healthier than ever.

Anthony Cronin said that every poem is a gift, every good poem a miracle. Writing this book has brought many miracles my way. Each woman's poetry has the hallmarks of hard work, persistence, courage, belief in the self and acknowledgement of the gift. If I found, at times, my energies were flagging, I turned to the poems for sustenance.

This is a very exciting time for Irish poetry and despite many problems associated with "the poetry business" it is a time of hope. Confident, powerful and important voices continue to emerge each year. Ireland's women poets have many differences, and have an innate sense of things being too various to stand accused of having either singular or insular views of themselves as poets or of their poetry. It is ultimately their business to write and to write as well as possible. It is not, in my view, the responsibility of the artist to be a social commentator or a politician. I believe the artist's function is to make art and to share it with the world. I offer this book as a record of such making and sharing.

Joan McBreen
Tuam, County Galway
November 1999

Poets AND Poetry

*Asterisk beside Poetry Collection in 'Poets and Poetry'
denotes collection is published in pamphlet form.*

Nuala Archer
(1955-)

 Poet and anthologist. Born to Irish parents in Rochester, New York. Studied Anglo-Irish literature at Trinity College, Dublin in 1977-1978 and taught in Ireland and the United States while working towards her Ph.D. which she received from the University of Wisconsin at Milwaukee. She edited the Winter 1986 special issue of *The Midland Review* in which she collected the work of more than forty Irish women writers. Describing herself as both an immigrant and an emigrant, Archer's poetry threads together the disparate people and contradictory events of her life as a young girl in Latin, Central and North America and as a young woman in Ireland. She has won several prizes including a first at Listowel Writers' Week and the Patrick Kavanagh Award in 1980. She lived for some years in Cleveland, Ohio, where she taught and was Director of the Poetry Center at Cleveland State University. She is at present studying visual arts and theatre arts in Jerusalem.

POETRY COLLECTIONS

Whale on the Line. (1981). Dublin, Gallery Press.
Two Women, Two Shores. (1989). Baltimore, New Poets Series / Galway, Salmon Publishing.
The Hour of Pan / amá. (1992). Galway, Salmon Publishing.
Pan / amá, a chapbook. (1992). New York, Red Dust.
From a Mobile Home. (1995). Galway, Salmon Publishing.

THE LOST GLOVE IS HAPPY

Is it in the terminal I left
the brown, rabbit-fur-lined gloves
made in Taiwan? Gloves
I've worn in Ireland.
Gloves that kept my fingers
warm walking the bitter cold
coastline of Bull Island
with Howth and her necklace
of lights in the background.
Gloves lost now between Stillwater,
Oklahoma and Lubbock, Texas
on the way to see my mother.

Come, she said, I'm in
the midst of desolation. Come.
Take Southwest Airlines, past
Love Field. I'll be waiting
for you. I'll be waiting.

And in the mall, when I got
to Lubbock, arrived to embrace
my mother in desolation, she had
me strip, try on outfit
after outfit – sweaters, trousers,
skirts, shirts, shorts, slips
and blouses – to see like
Mary, Mary, quite contrary,
how does your garden, my garden,
grow? She in her mid-fifties
and I at the cliff-edge of
twenty-nine. My mother had me
fly to Lubbock and on the way
I lost my rabbit–
fur-lined gloves. When I got
there, when I arrived, when

I reached desolation, my mother
alone, in the middle of crazy
cottonfields, my mother in
desolation, I reached her,
I travelled to her,
to desolation, and in desolation
we were as lost as any
two mismatched gloves and
for a few moments we relaxed, lost
and strangely happy,
in the Lubbock Mall, without
labels stripped to our bones.

Leland Bardwell

(1928-)

Poet, novelist and dramatist. Born in India of Irish parents, she grew up in Leixlip, County Kildare. She now lives in County Sligo. A member of Aosdána, she founded the literary magazine *Cyphers* with Eiléan Ní Chuilleanáin, Macdara Woods and Pearse Hutchinson. She has published novels, stories and poems and has had a number of plays produced. Although her first collection of poetry did not appear until 1970, she was already an established Irish poet, having published widely in periodicals throughout the 1960s. She continues to write and to support and encourage young and emerging writers in Ireland. Leland Bardwell is poetry editor of the Irish journal *Force 10*.

POETRY COLLECTIONS

The Mad Cyclist. (1970). Dublin, New Writers Press.
The Fly and the Bed Bug. (1984). Dublin, Beaver Row Press.
Dostoevsky's Grave – New and Selected Poems. (1991).
    Dublin, Dedalus Press.
The White Beach. (1998). County Clare, Salmon Publishing.

TWO LESSONS IN ANATOMY: YORK STREET, DUBLIN

Lesson I – i.m. The X Case.

The father of the pregnant girl
has lost his temper – their bodies
reflected in the armour of rush hour traffic.
Two people from one kitchen.
She rubs her eyes like a cat
polishing its face with a single paw.
His anger spins from the bones of his shoulders
with the crescendo of his curses.

She backs away, knocking into students,
bruising her ankle on the pedal of a bike.
She will go to that nowhere place
where decisions bang around in her head.
I wonder will she remember the time
the moth was banging against the electric bulb
and how she climbed on that wobbly chair
to cup the insect in her palm
to throw it from the open window.

Lesson II

The woman upstairs is being beaten.
Her screams jangle across the street
where windows in the College of Surgeons
black out one by one. Students
are filtering home to their digs
in Rathmines or Ranelagh
and the air is left untroubled
by the cry for help
that no lessons in anatomy can fathom.

Sara Berkeley

(1967-)

Poet, short story writer and novelist. Born in Dublin and educated at Trinity College, Dublin and at the University of California at Berkeley. Her first collection of poetry appeared when she was nineteen and was shortlisted for both the Irish Book Awards and *The Sunday Tribune* Arts Awards. Writing of her work, Paul Durcan said: "For me, Sara Berkeley is the most naturally gifted poet to emerge in Ireland since Michael Hartnett in 1960." Her themes include love, family relationships, exile, and loneliness. Her use of language is highly charged, demonstrating faithfully her true poetic ear.

POETRY COLLECTIONS

Penn. (1986). Dublin, The Raven Arts Press /
   Saskatchewan, Thistledown Press.
Home-Movie Nights. (1989). Dublin, The Raven Arts Press /
   Saskatchewan, Thistledown Press.
Facts about Water – New and Selected Poems. (1994). Dublin,
   New Island Books / Newcastle upon Tyne: Bloodaxe /
   Saskatchewan: Thistledown Press.

EMERGENCE

It was there all along, great peace,
I wear it again, I turn around in it.

What changes inside when the spark lights,
the fizz of a match coming up,
candles growing their yellow robes.

Curled up cottonball alone and warm,
at sea, rowing sporadically,
it feels like shipwreck and being found,
it feels like round rings falling into round.

On Limantour beach
I pay for concealment with dollars of sand,
birds fly the razor breaks of the waves,
I can find what I placed in the dark
I can dive by the light of Venus.

I like where I am sitting now,
but at your door I got shy,
left after knocking lightly.
One day you might hold me

in your piano hands
life all arpeggios and resolving chords.

Jean Bleakney

(1956-)

Poet and editor. Born in Newry, County Down. She was educated at Queen's University, Belfast where she worked as a biochemist for eight years. A member of the QUB Creative Writing Workshop, her poetry has been published in *Poetry Ireland Review*, *Brangle*, *The Rialto* and *Verse*. A runner-up in the Patrick Kavanagh Awards in 1997, *The Ripple Tank Experiment* is her first collection. She is assistant editor of the literary magazine Brangle. The British poet Carol Rumens has said that her poems belong to neither "the hedge school of workshop realism, nor to *l'Écriture Féminine*. They derive from their native place but are not circumscribed by it." Bleakney is aware of the complexity of being a poet and a woman in Northern Ireland.

POETRY COLLECTION

The Ripple Tank Experiment. (1999). Belfast, Lagan Press.

A WOMAN OF OUR TIMES

I wish you wouldn't look at me
as if to say *It's a tip, this place.*
There must be six week's Sunday papers
on that sofa. You couldn't find room
to butter a slice of bread . . .
you wouldn't want to put
a slice of bread on that worktop.
Would you ever consider hoovering?
I wish you'd think before you look.

I wish you'd BLINK instead and see
a Woman of Our Times
– a dedicated scientist
employing all of her resources
in the absence of outside funding
– a physicist painstakingly unravelling
the Second Law of Thermodynamics;
almost touching base in Chaos Theory
– a woman up to her eyes in entropy.

Eavan Boland

(1944-)

 Poet, critic and essayist. Born in Dublin. A leading contemporary poet, she was educated in London and New York and at Trinity College, Dublin where she received a degree in English and Classics. The publication of *New Territory*, her first collection in 1967, marked the arrival of an important and original voice. in 1968 she was awarded the Macauley Fellowship in Poetry and is a member of Aosdána. Her poetry explores the experience of domesticity, motherhood, suburbia and women's lives. These themes, together with her idea of the Irish nation as a construct from which she felt alienated, have provided contemporary Irish poetry with the figure of woman as a complex self within her own poems. Her essays on such themes have been collected and published in her book *Object Lessons: The Life of The Woman and the Poet in Our Time*. She has been awarded many prizes nationally and internationally for her poetry. Several of her collections have been British Poetry Book Society Choices. She is currently Professor of Poetry at Stanford University, California, USA, a position previously held by Denise Levertov and Adrienne Rich. The richness and strength of her poems have been a gift not alone to Irish poetry but to the very voice of her country.

POETRY COLLECTIONS

New Territory. (1967). Dublin, Allen Figgis.
The War Horse. (1975). Dublin, Arlen House /
    London, Victor Gollancz. (1975).
In Her Own Image. (1980). Dublin, Arlen House.
Night Feed. (1982). Dublin, Arlen House / London and Boston,
    Marion Boyars / Manchester, Carcanet Press. (1994).

The Journey and Other Poems. (1986). Dublin, Arlen House /
  Manchester, Carcanet Press. (1987).
Selected Poems. (1989). Manchester, Carcanet Press.
Outside History. (1990). Manchester, Carcanet Press.
Outside History: Selected Poems, 1980-1990. (1990). New York,
  Norton.
In a Time of Violence. (1994). Manchester, Carcanet Press /
  New York, Norton.
Collected Poems. (1995). Manchester, Carcanet Press.
An Origin Like Water: Collected Poems, 1967-1987. (1997).
  New York and London, Norton.
The Lost Land. (1998). Manchester, Carcanet Press / New York
  and London, Norton.

THE BLOSSOM

A May morning.
Light starting in the sky.

I have come here
after a long night.
Its senses of loss.
Its unrelenting memories of happiness.

The blossom on the apple tree is still in shadow,
its petals half-white and filled with water at the core,
in which the freshness and secrecy of dawn are stored
even in the dark.

How much longer
will I see girlhood in my daughter?

In other seasons
I knew every leaf on this tree.
Now I stand here
almost without seeing them

and so lost in grief
I hardly notice what is happening
as the light increases and the blossom speaks,
and turns to me
with blonde hair and my eyebrows and says –

imagine if I stayed here,
even for the sake of your love
what would happen to the summer?
To the fruit?

Then holds out a dawn-soaked hand to me,
whose fingers I counted at birth
years ago.

And touches mine for the last time.

And falls to earth.

Rosita Boland

(1965-)

Poet, journalist and travel writer. Born in Ennis, County Clare and educated at Trinity College, Dublin. She travelled extensively in Australia and worked for two years in London, later living in the West of Ireland. The poems in her first collection *Muscle Creek* reflect her experiences and ideas as poet/traveller through these different landscapes. Her translations from the Irish of Cathal Ó Searcaigh appeared in *The Bright Wave: An Tonn Gheal*, which received An Duais Bhord na Gaeilge and was the Poetry Ireland Choice in the year it was published. She received a Bursary in Literature from the Arts Council and in 1997 won *The Sunday Tribune* Hennessy Award for First Fiction. She now lives in Dublin where she works as a journalist for *The Irish Times*.

POETRY COLLECTION

Muscle Creek. (1991). Dublin, The Raven Arts Press.

DIAMONDS

The Tsarina knew
That some darkness was seeping ever closer.
In the uneasy stillness of their winter palace,
The Romanov women tried to prepare themselves
For whatever lay ahead.

Whispering together one silent dawn, their needles
Moving like splinters of light, they ripped open
Their silk and whalebone corsets,
Secreting diamonds along those many seams.

That same day,
Alexandra wrote in her diary
Olga and I arranged our medicines.
They thought they were ready, prepared
For an uncertain future, their valuables
Safely concealed against curve of breast
And hollow of heart.

The Tsarina did not know they had created
A bright filigree of betrayal: grotesque armour.
When the Bolsheviks came later that day,
Their bullets ricocheted off the diamonds.
After a while, they took up bayonets.

Eva Bourke

(1946-)

Poet, translator, editor, teacher. Born in West Germany, she has been living in Galway for many years. She works as a teacher and translator and has contributed to several German language publications of Irish poetry and literature. A member of the Galway Writers' Workshop since 1981, she has also been editor of 'Writing in the West', *The Connacht Tribune's* literary page. She received an Arts Council Bursary in 1996. Widely published in Ireland and abroad, her work has been translated into Swedish, Dutch, Italian, Romanian, Flemish and French. She has written critical articles on Irish and European poets in many journals and magazines. Her translations of the German poet Elisabeth Borchers will appear in *The Poetry Europe Series* (Dedalus Press) and she is currently working on a fourth collection of poetry. She has published two anthologies of Irish poetry in German translation: *Hundsrose* (1994) and *With Green Ink / Mit grüner Tinte* (1996). Her first two collections are illustrated by Jay Murphy, the painter and graphic artist. In her poems she crosses and re-crosses the boundaries, real and imaginary, between Europe and Ireland, always bringing her passionate vision and humanity to her reader with directness and clarity.

POETRY COLLECTIONS

Gonella. (1985). Galway, Salmon Publishing.
Litany For the Pig. (1989). Galway, Salmon Publishing.
Spring in Henry Street. (1996). Dublin, The Dedalus Press.

FROM: BERLIN NOTEBOOK

III – The Nightsinger

When our insomniac neighbour finally stops pacing,
the last cars slip into anchorage,
the last windows erase themselves
from the *Gründerzeit* facades opposite,

when night rains fall from the top tiers
of the summer theatre above Berlin
and each street lamp swims
in a wavery orange halo,

when all alarms are silenced,
the night is a great ear pressed close
to the heart of the city, and we sleep
high up under a pre-war roof

with nothing between us
and the vast outdoor auditorium,
its aisles and mute orchestra pit,
but a few bricks, planks and tiles,

we often wake after he's already gone past
a block or two, his voice still palming our dreams:
a full bass or baritone, the right touch
of vibrato, operatic but not excessively so,

light in the high notes: *Tosca*,
Il Trovatore, *The Magic Flute*,
a solo melody rising up and descending again
past firewalls, chimneys and gutters,

past the assembled polished utensils of the night.
We listen, the very houses bend and listen
to his voice coming from beyond parks
and bunkers, concert halls,

high rises, abattoirs, spaghetti junctions,
weaving in and out of the hem of darkness,
crossing the old divisions, losses, hopes, and the new.
In the gods, we think of him testing the freedom of the city

with each breath, each crescendo, think of blue
water rising to our attic and sweeping us
all the way to Brazil. We've heard him before,
here and there, turning up at exactly the hour

when ears are most receptive; you recall
hymns trailing round Boston Common at 3 a.m.,
barely audible above the ocean howl
of traffic, his pilgrim's zeal unquelled by police sirens;

once at Berlin Ostkreuz, Tristan on a bench between tracks
going all the way to middle B
beside himself with potion and desire,
and not long ago by the Eglinton canal, you swear,

you overheard him sing the Mikado in a scruffy overcoat
to an audience of waterfowl.
Call him a lunatic, you say, but unless you know
he's still wandering the city to his own song till daybreak

as though he were the guardian of our sleep
you can't feel right in a place.
Unless you know that he still has the freedom
to sing as pleases him, and we to listen.

Máire Bradshaw

(1943-)

Poet. Born in Limerick and educated at Laurel Hill Convent, she lives in Cork where she is a founding member of the Cork Women's Poetry Circle and Tigh Fhilí (Poets' House). Bradshaw's poetry is included in the ground-breaking anthology *The Box Under the Bed* (1986), a collection of writing from the Cork women writers which received the encouragement of Eavan Boland following a workshop she led, celebrating Cork 800 in 1985. Bradshaw runs workshops, organises readings and is active in the feminist movement in Cork. Her work has been translated into German and French. She represented the Cork Federation of Women's Organisations and the Cork Women's Poetry Circle at the Women's Forum in Huairou and at the United Nations Women's Conference in Beijing, China. Her poem *First Citizen/ Free Woman* was commissioned for the conferring of the Freedom of Cork City on President Mary Robinson.

POETRY COLLECTIONS

Instinct. (1988). Cork, Inksculptors Limited.
high time for all the marys. (1992). Cork and London,
    Inksculptors Limited.

EURYDICE

in tahilla by the bog lake
she watches two wild swans
on a lake of rich gold leaves

her face grows young
as it ripples through
rush and bamboo shoot

his voice calls time
she turns her head

EURYDICE

à tahilla près du lac de la tourbière
elle observe deux cygnes sauvages
sur un lac de feuilles aux riches couleur d'or

son visage rajeunit
à mesure qu'il ondoie à travers
les joncs et les pousses de bambous

la voix de l'homme crie il est l'heure
elle tourne la tête

Deirdre Brennan

(1934-)

Poet, fiction writer and dramatist. Born in Dublin, she was educated in the Ursuline Convent in Thurles. Studied English and Latin in University College, Dublin where she received a BA degree and a Higher Diploma in Education. Her poetry has been published in *Poetry Ireland, The Works, Windows* and *Writing Women*. A collection of her short stories in Irish won *Duais Bhord na Gaeilge* at Writers' Week in Listowel in 1996. Her stories in English have been broadcast on Cork Campus Radio. She won an Oireachtas prize for Radio Drama in 1994 and a drama series *Go to Blazes* was broadcast by RTÉ Radio 1 in the same year. A lyric poet, love, responsibility and nature are her common themes.

POETRY COLLECTIONS

I reilig na mban rialta. (1984). Baile Átha Cliath, Coiscéim.
Scothanna geala (1989). Baile Átha Cliath, Coiscéim.
Thar cholbha na mara. (1993). Baile Átha Cliath, Coiscéim.

CEILTEANAS

Amuigh faoi na labáin, faoi na plobáin
Mar a bhfaigheann an dreoilín teaspaigh
Is an drúchtín móna dídean
Codlaíonn seandachtaí rúnda:
Tírdhreacha imithe ar ceal orainn;
Claíocha críche is teorainneacha cianda;
Áitribh, torchairí is cnámha ár sinsir;

Na cluainte bhíodh á n-ingilt
Ag caoraigh, eallaigh is gabhair;
Síolta eornan is cruithneachtana is féir.

Láimh liom, adhlachta fád' ghealchraiceann
Codalíonn seandachtaí ganfhiosacha eile –
Cladráin is feoráin is diamhraí dubha
Mar a dtéann tú sa bhfraoch ar luas nó ar mire;
Láimh liom faoi fhuanbhrat do ghealchraicinn
Luíonn anamdhreach narbh éigin dom a shamhlú,
Iomairí as a bpéacann na sean síolta
Nár mhian liom a mbarra a bhaint.

COVERTURE

Out under the wetlands, the squelchy places
Where the grasshopper and sundew plant
Find sanctuary, sleeps a secret geography;
Landscapes long lost to sight;
Boundary hedges, remote confines;
Habitations, possessions, and bones of our ancestors;
The meadows grazed by their cattle, sheep and goats;
Their seeds of barley, wheat and grass
Inert under old headlands.

Beside me, buried under your bright skin
Sleeps another secret geography –
Stony river beds, wild shores, black recesses
Where sooner or later you escape me.
Beside me concealed by your bright skin,
Lies a soulscape I would rather not imagine
Where drills sprout old seeds
Whose harvest I would prefer not to gather.

trans. author.

Lucy Brennan

(1931-)

 Poet. Born in Dublin in 1931, she was educated and grew up in Cork. She emigrated to Montreal, Canada in 1957 and now lives in Whitby, Ontario. In 1992 she received a Master of Fine Arts Degree in Creative Writing from Warren Wilson College in North Carolina. Her poetry has been published in: *Poetry Canada Review*, *The Antigonish Review*, *Poetry Toronto*, *Canadian Women Studies*, *Poetry Ireland Review*, *The Sunday Tribune*, *The Salmon*, *Stet* and *Honest Ulsterman*. She has read her poetry widely in Canada and in Dublin for Poetry Ireland. The poet Eleanor Wilner has said of her work: "the cost of freedom is counted, not in complaint but in the consoling, heart-rousing measures of song."

POETRY COLLECTION

Migrants All. (1999). Toronto, watershedBooks.

THE WEDDING DRESS

I found it folded away:
a puff of peach-coloured cloud
with those tiered flounces
that define the Twenties.

Even at my slimmest
I couldn't try it on:
The white tulle had aged delicately,
fragile like everything about her.

One's mother as a bride
is inconceivable.
Was she once full of confidence
in herself, in life?

His life had been bleak
until she stepped into it:
his *aisling*, his dream-maiden,
defying translation.

When his songs deserted him
she was parched for want of such music.
Soon distance pushed its way
into the silences that grew between them.

Then she folded away
that cloud of tulle.

Heather Brett

(1956-)

Poet and editor. Born in Newfoundland and raised in County Antrim, she trained as a fashion designer in York Street Art College, Belfast. While living in Dublin she met Leland Bardwell who introduced her to contemporary poetry and encouraged her to publish her own work. Her first book *Abigail Brown* won the 1992 Brendan Behan Memorial Prize and in the same year she was awarded an Arts Council Bursary. Living in County Cavan, she has been editor of *Windows Publications* since 1992. The natural world, children, memory and sexuality are among the themes she chooses to explore in her poetry, which appears regularly in magazines and anthologies in Ireland, Romania and Canada.

POETRY COLLECTIONS

Abigail Brown. (1991). Galway, Salmon Publishing.
The Touch-Maker. (1994). Cavan, Alternative Publishing /
    Toronto, Litterae.

BLOODTHIRST

The theatrics are over
we've finished
our mad naked tango
through the abattoir
the long pointed knives
inflicting their fair share of pain.
Why is it never easy?
Why is it always an eye for an eye,
one wound for the other?
Who are we really playing to?
is there some apparent applause
in the background, spurring us on
the audience all the dead replicas of ourselves?
The battle always becomes more
than the issue that began it,
moves too swiftly out of control,
imperative to an end.
We set the stage
criss-cross the ring with lines
over which the other steps at their peril.
Many times I've felt more like the bull
than the matador,
many times I've thought of that cool white flag
waving in the wind.
But, like you, I can't give in,
back down, lose face
just one word and the red blood-
thirst rages again.
But sometimes, *only* sometimes
I catch a faint whisper –
who's pulling my strings,
slipping their hand inside the glove?
Even deserted and clean
the abattoir still smells of blood.

Patricia Burke Brogan

(1932-)

Poet, painter, playwright, graphic artist. Born in County Clare, she was educated at the St. Louis Convent, Balla, County Mayo. She trained as a primary teacher at Carysfort College, Dublin. Her short stories and poems have been published in Ireland, the USA and Italy. Exhibited widely in Ireland, her paintings and graphics have also appeared in exhibitions in Spain, Japan and Hawaii. *Eclipsed*, her stage play, premiered at the Punchbag Theatre in Galway and went on to the 1992 Edinburgh Fringe Festival where it won the Scotsman Fringe First Award and was short-listed for the London Independent Theatre Award. The USA premiere of the play won the Moss Hart Theatre Award in 1994. Awarded an Arts Council Grant in 1993, her poetry and prose won prizes at many literary festivals in Ireland. Drawing from the world of images, from European and Classical Art, from mythic symbols and shapes, her painting turned to writing, in particular to poetry and she combined both in her first collection. The themes of pain and personal revelation are handled with courage and integrity in all of this multi-talented artist's work but nowhere with such intelligence and sensitivity as in her poetry. She lives in Galway city where she is a member of the Galway Writers' Workshop. Work-in-progress includes new plays, *Harness The Stars* and *The Generous Imposter*, and she is writing a new collection of poetry.

POETRY COLLECTION

Above The Waves Calligraphy. (1994). Galway, Salmon Publishing.

PATTERNS

Rhythm of water
pleats and folds
on river mouth
at Labasheeda.

      Pulse of jet-planes
      from Moscow, from Boston
      shudder above Ardnacrusha.

Rhythm of stone axe
on straight-grained poplar
shaped and carved this canoe
seven thousand years ago.

      Heartbeat of a child,
      swells from a womb-canoe
      below Saint's Island.

In Kiladysert
the child plays
with mud-patterns
from the estuary.
With a blue crayon
she makes word-patterns,
finds a river poem.

Catherine Byron

(1947-)

Poet, prose-writer and reviewer. Born in London to an Irish mother and English father. Lived in Belfast from 1948 to 1964 and was educated there and at Oxford. In 1984 she received an East Midlands Arts Bursary. Her prose volume *Out of Step: Pursuing Seamus Heaney to Purgatory* (1992), is both a powerful tribute to Heaney and a critical statement of the way she interprets his poetry as invoking but silencing the feminine. In her poetry she deals with the dilemma of exile, her love for the landscape and history of Ireland. She also explores her difficulties with the links between the feminine and masculine in herself, in her relationship to patriarchal Catholicism and in Seamus Heaney's work. Byron teaches writing and medieval literature at The Nottingham Trent University.

POETRY COLLECTIONS

Settlements. (1985). Durham, Taxus Press.
The Fat-Hen Field Hospital, Poems 1985-1992. (1993).
    Bristol, Loxwood Stoneleigh.
Settlements and Samhain. (1993). Bristol, Loxwood Stoneleigh.
The Three She's. (1994). Dusseldorf, Verlag der Handzeichen.
The Getting of Vellum. (1999), Leicester, UK, Blackwater Press /
    County Clare, Salmon Publishing.

MINDING YOU

You say you want to go home.
Shall I drive you there, one last time?
Across the water,
over the Bog of Allen
and the great Shannon divide –
home, to Ballinahistle?
To the field that has been in your head
from seventeen years old
to seventy-seven,
the years you have been away?

This is the in-field, just over
the parkeen wall, and past
the ancient stand-alone thorn
and the line of damson trees.
Young Tony, your brother's son,
will show us again
the mounds and eskers of stones
he and his nephews have picked
like hard grey potatoes
from the field's ploughed lines.
Is it never done with,
the stone-picking in this field?

Seventy years ago,
your first grown-up work:
October potato-picking,
then the second
months-long harvest of stones
as winter's rains revealed them,
crop after crop.

I would take you now
and put cold stones in your hands
at the in-field's sodden edge,
lead you into December's
sticky furrows,
if touch, and step
could somehow bring you home,
here, in England,
to your own lost mind.

Louise C. Callaghan

(1948-)

Poet and teacher. Born in Dublin and educated at University College, Dublin where she studied English and Spanish. Travelled widely in India, the USA, Majorca, Spain, Mexico and Ecuador, South America. She worked for some time in the 1980s as an editor for Arlen House: The Women's Press, Dublin. She spent 1995-1996 in Oaklands, Northern California where, together with facilitating writers' workshops for women, she took creative writing classes at the University of California at Berkeley. In her poetry Callaghan meshes a personal and universal world view, drawing on memory and relationships. Celebrating love, she writes with a lyric voice.

POETRY COLLECTION

The Puzzle-Heart. (1999). County Clare, Salmon Publishing.

THE PALATINE DAUGHTER MARRIES A CATHOLIC

I am a stranger in your country,
it is my hair,
unlike anyone else's.
You say it is the wrong kind of water
to wash brass-coloured hair,
use rain-water, I suppose!

I was taken from my Rhine-watered land,
washed up on someone else's tide,
a pale corpse: 'cordially hated by the natives.'
You said I was a lily –
that my skin reminded you of beeswax.

Now I have not the least sense of place,
never wear the same colour twice,
work wherever I find myself. Read
as if I don't exist, make the land ripen,
the timeless hillside a furze of apple-blossom,
the compost dark and smell-less
by constant turning – till I'm summoned
by marriage like a piece of furniture
to the nearby barony
the other side of Seefin.

Our bibles are all buried now,
my back is against the light of Glenosheen.
I have not given birth in this land.
And when you say you love me
I wonder what it is you think you love,
the land of no return?
the River of the Morningstar?
the warm-walled kitchen garden,
the flax patches of blue haze?
or is it the grey canvas shoes
beneath my strange palatine bed?

Yes, I will let you come to me,
I am all yours, only don't expect
me to talk of love, even in my sleep,
nor honour your people's oppositions
when here is no safe haven
for settler or dispossessed.

Siobhán Campbell

(1962-)

Poet. Born in Dublin, she was educated at the Loreto Convent, Dublin and at University College, Dublin. She was encouraged and published by David Marcus, novelist and literary editor who founded, in 1967 'New Irish Writing,' the literary page of *The Irish Press*. She worked in book publishing for many years, first with Butler Sims and then Wolfhound Press. She has been involved with this press for fifteen years and has been a director for a decade, working for them now from the USA.. She was a member of various writers' groups including the Dublin Writers' Workshop, Voicefree and Palmer's Circle. Her poetry has been published in many magazines and journals including *Cyphers*, *Orbis*, *Poetry Ireland* and *The Sunday Tribune*. It has been anthologised in *Pillars of the House* (1988), *Irish Poetry Now* (1993) and *Ireland's Women: Writings Past and Present* (1994). She spent time in New York in 1992 and gave readings in Sin É and the Nuyorican Poets Café. Her themes include family, love, ageing and death. She reveals herself in her poems, often with humour, sometimes in a harsher light.

POETRY COLLECTION

The Permanent Wave. (1996). Belfast, The Blackstaff Press.

THE HALTING

Love can stop though its stopping may be slow.
This time it is a shock, a real surprise.
Yet it is difficult to let you go.

What bound us is asunder now, although
Neither of us quite recognised –
Love can stop though its stopping may be slow.

I've felt the chill of my resentment grow,
Fed by past hopes and present pride
Yet it is difficult to let you go.

I look at you and wonder if you know
That our journey's over, we've arrived.
Love stops but there's no whistle to blow,

Nothing to make a fitting finish, show
Us to be kind and just, not to have lied.
Yes, it is difficult to let you go.

How will I start, begin to tell you so,
Or should I pretend nothing has died?
It is so difficult to let you go.
Love can stop though its stopping may be slow.

Rosemary Canavan

(1949-)

 Poet, painter, teacher. Born in Scotland and has lived in Cork for many years. From her experience as a teacher of literacy at the prison on Spike Island, and from the Irish patriot John Mitchel's book *Jail Journal*, she found the theme for the long poem which is also the title of her first collection. This poem was shortlisted for the Vincent Buckley Poetry Prize at the University of Melbourne. She also read at the Cheltenham Literary Festival in 1995. She has been artist-in-residence at The Triskel Arts Centre, Cork. An accomplished painter, she describes herself as somebody who "paints from love and writes from need," considering the mesh of both to come from the same source. She continues to teach and to publish poetry and is a member of the Cork Women's Poetry Circle. Her poetry is imbued with her struggles as a working mother and the feminist consciousness of a new generation of Irish women.

POETRY COLLECTIONS

The Island. (1994). Oregon, USA, Story Line Press.

SEA WIDOW

After the Piper Alpha disaster

In the night he comes to me
– shut out the dark night –
my dead love, burning and bloody,

become dark, terrible, a lover
riding the wings of morning,
his hair streaming in the cool wind,

the oil
flaring in great gouts below him,
a corolla of pain
casting lurid colour
on the dark water,

and the roar
as the rig went up
"O we knew, we knew," he cried
"as we shielded our faces
from the white wall of flame,
and the sudden agony, gone again
as the dark quiet suddenly came,"

so leave me, neighbours, friends,
women bearing tea and quiet talk
to soothe pain; it is
in the night, in the night
he comes to me.

Moya Cannon

(1956-)

Poet, teacher, editor. Born in Dunfanaghy, County Donegal in 1956 and educated at University College, Dublin and at Corpus Christi, Cambridge. She has lived for many years in Galway where she teaches traveller children. Her first collection, *Oar* (1990), received the Brendan Behan Memorial Prize and she gives readings widely in Ireland and abroad. Her poems are dialogues with the landscape, love poems and poems of mourning for the loss of the Irish language, many of which have been set to music by composers such as Jane O'Leary, Philip Martin and others. She was writer-in-residence at Trent University, Ontario in 1994-1995. She draws attention to the solace found in the articulation of human experience and she illustrates the great difference between English and Irish language, culture and mentality. Editor of *Poetry Ireland Review*, Nos. 45-48, she chose as themes for two of her issues "Poetry and Survival" and "The Sacred and The Secular," both of which reflect her own vision.

POETRY COLLECTIONS

Oar. (1990). Galway, Salmon Publishing.
The Parchment Boat. (1997). County Meath, The Gallery Press.

NIGHT

Coming back from Cloghane
in the sudden frost
of a November night,
I was ambushed
by the river of stars.

Disarmed by lit skies
I had utterly forgotten
this arc of darkness,
this black night
where the frost-hammered stars
were notes thrown from a chanter,
crans of light.

So I wasn't ready
for the dreadful glamour of Orion
as he struck out over Barr dTrí gCom
in his belt of stars.

At Gleann na nGealt
his bow of stars
was drawn against my heart.

What could I do?

Rather than drive into a pitch-black ditch
I got out twice,
leaned back against the car
and stared up at our windy, untidy loft
where old people had flung up old junk
they'd thought might come in handy,
ploughs, ladles, bears, lions, a clatter of heroes,
a few heroines, a path for the white cow, a swan
and, low down, almost within reach,
Venus, completely unfazed by the frost.

Ruth Carr

(1953-)

Poet, teacher, editor. Born in Belfast where she still lives. Her poems have appeared widely in journals and anthologies including *Map-Makers' Colours* (Nu-age Editions, Montreal, 1988), *Sleeping with Monsters* (Wolfhound, Dublin, 1990) and *Word of Mouth* (Blackstaff, Belfast, 1996). She wrote a monologue, *What the Eye Doesn't See*, which was commissioned and performed by Point Fields Theatre Company in Belfast and the Glasgow Mayfest in 1994. She works part-time as a tutor in adult education and has assisted many writing groups in publishing their own work. Under the name Hooley, she edited *The Female Line*, a pioneering anthology of poetry and fiction by Northern Irish women writers. She is currently associate editor of the *Honest Ulsterman* poetry magazine.

POETRY COLLECTION

There is a House. (1999). County Donegal, Summer Palace Press.

WE SHARE THE SAME SKIN
for my mother

We shared the same skin, your touch
home to my body. To grow up
I built walls, defining
where you ended and I began.

It was a child sulking to shut
you out. You waited, a quiet
stream for me to surface in.
That's where to find you now –

hunkered down on a river bank
needle or pencil in hand, sometimes
pins in your mouth, sometimes humming,
or leant against some stubborn

wind-spent tree. You showed me that
obvious thing – that under the skin
there's human, that dressing up is
a game fit only for children.

That obvious thing that nobody does –
you did it most times,
shared your skin with so many,
I needed to know you loved

me more than any old refugee.
I walled up inside, let my body
go begging for crumbs like poor Tom,
a craving that couldn't find centre.

But we shared the same skin
and when yours grew too tired
and too yellow to care –
with a child of my own but still

not grown up, I couldn't let go
until prodigal waters burst
mortar from brick, I broke through
to your salt-bedded river.

We share the same skin, my daughter
and me. She's building walls
to define where I end
and she can make a beginning.

Juanita Casey

(1925-)

Poet, novelist and short-story writer. Born in England the daughter of an Irish travelling woman who died when she was born. Her early life was divided between boarding schools and the circus and she became horse master for Robert Brothers' Circus. She left school at the age of thirteen, to train horses and zebras. Her love of animals, in particular horses, permeates her writing which she came to later in her life. She has also been a farmer and a trainer and breeder of horses. In the 1970s she was a reviewer for the *Irish Press* and published poetry and short stories in many Irish and British journals. In 1966 J.M. Dent (Great Britain) published a collection of her short stories *Hath Rain a Father*, now out of print. She lives in Devon and is working on another collection of poetry, short stories and her autobiography. The dust jacket of her first collection *Horse by the River* carries this quote from the author: "Let me say, as a poet, I am much taken up with the thing of being a woman." Her poetry bears out this statement.

POETRY COLLECTIONS

Horse by the River. (1968). Dublin, The Dolmen Press.
Eternity Smith and Other Poems. (1985). Portlaoise, The Dolmen Press.

ZEN AND NOW

Reading Basho
Under fox-shared bracken,
Warblers distilling song
Out of early morning rain
And three swans pulsing
For a silver landfall;
That would please him–
Who'd have thought
Swans farted–
Plop!
The old pond and that famous frog ...
Now we hear
It's a wrong translation.
Plop! an illusion.
Illustration: a buffalo,
Horned like a boomerang,
Carrying Grandpa
Rump-perched like a tinker;
In another, facing backward,
(All Desire Gone)
Like a kid on an obliging donkey.
A blank page–
'The Cow and Sage Quite Gone Out of Sight' ...
Round the bend
Or through the gate,
The last water-buffalo
(With or without Sage),
The hundred Pythagorean oxen –
(The I-Ching: 'No Blame')
Or Mullingar heifer –
The cows of the world
Are the same;
Huffing strings of drooling effs,
Blatting flies with sinewy
Kelp-tails,
Pocketing the World

Through half-mast, megaphone ears,
And roundly gathering it in
With fish-bowl stares
Through gobstopper eyeballs;
'Quite out of Sight'?
Philosophy
Has forgotten the inevitable
Cowpat.

Glenda Cimino

(1946-)

Poet and editor. Born in the United States, Glenda Cimino moved to Ireland in 1972. In 1980 she co-founded Beaver Row Press in Dublin and was responsible for bringing many emerging and more established poets into print in new collections. In 1986 her first book of poetry was published by her own press. She worked for a Florida newspaper in recent years and is again based in Dublin. She has co-produced and directed plays for community radio under the auspices of WrAP (Writers and Artists Production Cooperative), published haiku in *Haiku Spirit*, and has published her poetry on the internet with the Dublin Writers Workshop and won honorable mention in the Tallaght Clothesline Productions competition in 1998 for her poem "St. Brigid's Well." She was included in *Irish Poetry Now – Other Voices*, edited by Gabriel Fitzmaurice (1993). Her poetry draws on her life in the USA and her contrasting life in Ireland.

POETRY COLLECTION

Cicada. (1986). Dublin, Beaver Row Press.

WHAT THE COURT CLERK SAID

When I was a girl
the land was free
we had our houses
far apart
and rode horses.
there was no dam
and the river
flowed freely.
I never saw
a policeman
and a white man
seldom
which was often enough.
we spoke
our own beautiful
words.
today
our houses
are back to back
with cement in between
there are not so many
horses
the river is gone
there are many police
many white men
and many drunken Indians.
my children
go to school
they learn English
and forget
their own tongue.
I must work here
and my husband
is a policeman.

(Rosebud Reservation, South Dakota, 1970)

Anne Cluysenaar

(1936-)

Poet. Born in Brussels, Belgium of Belgian-Irish parents and educated in Britain and Ireland. She received a degree from Trinity College, Dublin and became an Irish citizen in 1961. She has lectured at Trinity College, Lancaster University and many other academic institutions in Britain. She withdrew from full-time academic life many years ago to concentrate on writing and painting. She teaches creative writing part-time at the University of Wales and gives readings and workshops at festivals and in schools. Co-founder and secretary of the Usk Valley Vaughan Association, she is poetry editor of *Scintilla 3*, the most recent edition of the UVVA's literary publication. In the 1960s and 1970s her poetry appeared in Irish publications such as *The Dubliner, The Dublin Magazine, Phoenix* and *The Irish Times*. Living in Wales, her poetry has appeared in *New Welsh Review, Poetry Review, Poetry Wales, Scintilla* and *The Literary Review*. She has written a short opera and songs for the composer Geoffrey Palmer. When her collection *Nodes* was published in Ireland by The Dolmen Press in 1971, Cluysenaar was considered a poet of elegance and importance at a time when few women poets were being given attention.

POETRY COLLECTIONS

Nodes, Selected Poems, 1960-1968. (1971). Dublin, The Dolmen Press.
Double Helix. (1982). Manchester, Carcanet Press.
Timeslips. (1997). Manchester, Carcanet Press.

A PRESENCE

I stood with my toes to the pool's margin
idly looking down, the gold of the mud
half-hidden by silvery flutters of water.
Then, as in a trick picture, a presence
emerged from the gold, pink-brown spots held fast
by invisible edges, a ghostly thickening.
Around it, the sunlit mud, two-dimensional, spotless.
I wondered, was it conscious (of me, that is)?
I leant a fraction forward. I must have crossed
some safety-barrier. Its judgement of my shape
changed: no longer a blundering passer-by,
one of the sheep, the donkey browsing rushes,
but something with intentions – a threatening intentness.

So it went, in a puff of mud, the convulsion
too fast to be seen, its after-image
(from before I tried to get too close,
which I carry with me) still motionless on the retina.

Susan Connolly

(1956-)

Poet. Born in Drogheda, County Louth. She studied Italian and Music at University College, Dublin. She has had poetry published in journals and magazines throughout Ireland and the UK. *Boann and Other Poems*, a selection of her work, appeared in the volume *How High the Moon* (1991) which was a prize-winning volume, the outcome of a project undertaken by Co-operation North and Poetry Ireland, with the support of the Calouste Gulbenkian Foundation (UK). Her themes are child-birth, mother-birth, woman-birth and earth-birth. Many of her most interesting and dramatic poems are influenced by her knowledge of Irish folklore and mythology. She acknowledges the work of Patricia Lysaght's 1986 book *The Banshee – The Irish Supernatural Death-Messenger* (Glendale Press). The composer Michael Holohan has set some of her poetry to music. In 1998 her sequence *Well Fever* appeared in *Stone and Tree Sheltering Water: An Exploration of Sacred and Secular Wells in County Louth* (Flax Mill Publications), a book she researched and wrote with Anne Marie Moroney.

POETRY COLLECTIONS

How High the Moon – Boann and Other Poems with *Sanctuary* by Catherine Phil MacCarthy. (1991). Dublin, Poetry Ireland / Co-operation North.
For the Stranger. (1993). Dublin, The Dedalus Press.

FOR THE STRANGER

1.

Pick up a ragged red leaf as you walk;
squeeze it in your right hand:
                              you'll feel
above rain and rivermist
the first handshake of a colder sun.

2.

Think of your soul as a red leaf
leaving its remote high branch
to drift until it lands
at the stranger's feet.
                    If she stoops
to pick up this ragged leaf,
what will she learn about you?

3.

'Of the million steps taken
since I first made my high-spirited
leap from child to woman –
find out what conclusion
my journey has led me to
                    by asking
what I still hope for.'

4.

'For thirty years I have been
trying to speak to you.
For fifteen I have worn
a mask like a thirst.
People are still beyond my reach,
this world too much a reflection
                    without source.'

5.

At first the stranger thinks
she has been dreaming.
Then her steps change direction.
She heard you,
is looking for you.

6.

In the same town
or a hundred miles away
you drop the ragged red leaf
and make for home, thinking:

'Now be reassured
you will meet the stranger, and begin
the only possible conversation
to quench your thirst of fifteen years.'

Roz Cowman

(1942-)

Poet and teacher. Born in Cork, she was educated at University College, Cork. She won the Arlen House/Maxwell House Award in 1982 and received an Irish Arts Council Bursary in the same year. In 1985 she won the Patrick Kavanagh Poetry Prize and has been widely published in Ireland, Britain and the USA. She teaches creative writing and is involved in Adult Education in the south-east of Ireland. Her short poems, written in free-verse, express the lived life of the poet, drawing for their imagery on myth and fairy-tales.

POETRY COLLECTION

The Goose Herd. (1989). Galway, Salmon Publishing.

DREAM OF THE RED CHAMBER

Red tides have filled
the estuary; dykes
are down; the land
of the two canals
is gone.

Old hill, if I tread
stepping-stones of black
bungalows back to the first
threshold, the dream
of a red room,

will you accept
my journey as a rite
of passage, and absorb me

as the hare mother absorbs
her foetus children
into her blood
when spring is stillborn,
and late frosts
salt the earth?

Vicki Crowley

(1940-)

 Poet and painter. Born in Malta, she was educated there and in England. Trained in Architectural Drawing, she has travelled extensively in Europe and Africa. As a painter, she has had many solo exhibitions internationally, including representing Ireland in the Trieste Collective. Her paintings and silk wall hangings are in public and private collections all over the world. Her first collection of poetry is illustrated with twenty-one examples of her artwork, both in colour and in black and white. John Behan RHA. has written of her poetry: "The poems speak directly to us ... They float like the Ghibli wind through the book, making words and images one." They can be best described as a personal diary of a life written by a visual artist at home with words. Vicki Crowley shares this combination of gifts with several other Irish contemporary women poets.

POETRY COLLECTION

Oasis in a Sea of Dust. (1992). Galway, Salmon Publishing.

THE NEW CANVAS

Stretched taut and pregnant
With its promise
Its gleaming surface throbs
With pristine power.
It is first forbidding
Then seductive,
Changing, moving
Like a great kaleidoscope,
Mirroring my inner thoughts.

It is the sea then the sky
It is an embrace, then a flower.
It is a child; it is night,
Hypnotic and compelling.
I succumb at last
And with deliberate strokes,
I lay the single colour
That feels so right
For now I know
With white on white,
That I shall always see
Into its emptiness.

Yvonne Cullen

(1966-)

 Poet and musician. Born in Dublin and educated in Santa Maria College, UCD and King's Inns where she studied Law. Instead of following a career in law, she turned to writing and music. She was awarded an Arts Council Scholarship to the Poets' House in 1994 and was a participant at the Eastern Washington University Summer School in 1995. A prizewinner in the Yorkshire International Open Poetry Competition and winner of the American Ireland Fund Award in 1997, she was one of five Irish poets chosen for a two week reading tour of Sicily in 1998. She gives readings, leads workshops and plays the cello for the pop band Northlight Razorblade! An adaptation of her first screenplay, *Letters to Ursula,* will be staged in Dublin in 1999. Poets John Burnside and Kerry Hardie have praised her poetry. Hardie has said: "Cullen's work has the hallmarks of an original, sensual and important poetic imagination." Displaying a subtle energy, these poems bring to modern Irish poetry a new and confident voice.

POETRY COLLECTION

Invitation To The Air. (1998). Dublin, iTaLiCs Press.

FOR WHILE WE'LL WRITE LETTERS, AND FOR WHEN WE WON'T

The heart commands,
the frost that gently captivates us ....
Paul Celan

Now I know enough
to see mid-morning.
Villages a white van leaps through.
A dream's speed has you in
clothes like yours –
from the wheel you turn towards me.
Strike of a match here, and sentence from you flares.

Or I've thought one of your kids' names:
vivid, he's licking chocolate powder
from browned lips; shrugs ....
the sheen and fall
of his hair like laughter
is virtually here –
in a Camera Obscura where we almost live,
an imagined river.

Here, the same
butterfly brings five, six times to rest on a garden table
her wrought metal legs,
dips her wings to each absolute angle.
And presence means seeing it,
the heat of a forearm.
Now what I keep is settling,
some natural way –
like logs on your roadsides.
Into change, without nostalgia;
the blue past branches in an afternoon
became the end of
a life in which I mightn't see you.

Now I'd see for a long time,
at times, the stay of a life maybe
some clearer width of after rain in my days.
The sentences' cut sods
not disappointing us
nor that the letters would never be
gazettes from the routines
of shoelaces, dinners.

The silence we moved to would be never silence.
If midges in gardens
rise, incandescent as laughs;
often, breezes would travel one's table, the other's windowsill.
What a small thing when we'd forget each other,
brother facing the blue facing the blackness.
The taps of the wings
of butterflies at take-off, these heartbeats:

uncountable, over.

Paula Cunningham

(1963-)

Poet and dentist. Born in Omagh, County Tyrone and educated at Loreto Convent, Omagh and Queen's University, Belfast where she studied dentistry (1981-1985). She began to write and publish her poetry in 1994 and was awarded an Irish Arts Council scholarship to attend the Eastern Washington University Summer School in Dublin in 1995. Her poetry has appeared in *Poetry Ireland Review*, *Podium*, *Women's Work*, *North* and *f/m magazine* and has been broadcast on Bangor Community Radio and BBC Radio 4. In 1998 she won The Poetry Business Book and Pamphlet Competition. She has given numerous readings in Northern and Southern Ireland and in England. Currently studying for a BA degree in Drama and English at Queen's University, Belfast, she works part-time as a dentist. Her first play *The Silver Wake* is being developed in conjunction with Tinderbox Theatre Company Belfast. Some of the poems in her collection *A Dog called chance* chart her response to the 1998 Omagh bombing. Paula Meehan has said of her work: "She has the formal gifts in abundance ... when her eye is on her native Ulster, magic and frightening things happen." Themes of memory, sexuality, love and loss permeate her poetry. She is one of Ulster's most innovative younger poets.

POETRY COLLECTION

A Dog called chance. (1999). Huddersfield, Smith / Doorstop Books.

SOMETIMES DANCING

Advance, retreat, the chandeliers are
hot tonight, their cut beads
bend the golden light like tears.

Advance, retreat, pass through, dance home.
Gallop. Swing with your partner. Change.
In her dream she is princess, pale

hair coiled in knots, she's trussed in whalebone,
small breasts thrust to touch the heavy choker
at her throat. Advance, retreat. She's been trained

for this, shoulders back, the particular
angle chin and throat describe, balancing
heavy books she thought were made

for practice, and later Mother's precious plates
from China. Sometimes, dancing, she'll force her eyes
up, back, till over the eyebrow's arch

she sees the golden drops, and the room
spins. She does not see
the men she dances with, though she feigns

attention, smiling. She feels
their hands long after they've passed on.
When she dances with Clara she holds tighter

than she should, pushes herself beyond
giddiness. Leans into her. A little.
Once in her dream, swinging,

their bodies locked together and they flew.
She woke to a crashing of plates, a tangle
of sheets in her narrow bed, the heart galloping.

Bríd Dáibhís

(1930-)

Poet and dramatist. Born near Portlaoise, she was educated in Mountmellick and entered a convent at the age of seventeen. Trained as a Primary teacher in Carysfort College, Dublin, she graduated in 1952. She studied Irish Literature in St. Patrick's College, Maynooth, 1972-1973. A prizewinner in 1966 when her poetry won the *Duais Chuimhneacháin 1916*, her poems have also been published in *Comhar, Feasta, An Sagart* and *An tUltach*. Although her poetic themes vary, the rope of Christianity is woven throughout. Echoes of old Irish monastic writing are found in dual images of nature and praising the Creator.

POETRY COLLECTIONS

Corrán gealaí. (1978). Baile Átha Cliath, Coiscéim.
Cosán na gréine. (1989). Baile Átha Cliath, Coiscéim.
Tráithnín Seirce. (1999). Baile Átha Cliath, Coiscéim.

LEACA

Shiúil mé an tóchar síos chun an tobair,
Ar leaca ársa na cistine;
Clochghainimh a dealbhadh fadó
Go foirm leaca i gcoiréal sa sliabh.
Leagadh le taobh a chéile
Ar Bhán Uí Riagáin iad,
Ina dteorainn tréan idir cosa is cré.

I gcaitheamh na mblianta
Trasnaíodh iad gan staonadh.
Rinceadh orthu i dtráth.
D'airigh siad tadhall na nglúine
Ar uair na hurnaí.
Ba tharstu a hiompraíodh
Cónraí mo shinsir.

Ach lá amháin, le teann faisin,
Cinneadh ar a n-ardú,
Agus deineadh bealach
Don stroighin is don lionóil.

Ach táid ar thaobh an tsléibhe arís,
Tá lom na gaoithe orthu.
Mar bhealach chun an tobair dóibh
Beidh cosa nua á satailt.

FLAGSTONES

I walked down the causeway to the well
On the ancient flagstones of the kitchen;
Sandstone fashioned long ago
To the shape of flags in a mountain quarry.
They were laid alongside each other
On Bawn Reagan
As stout boundary between feet and clay.

Over the years they were crossed continuously,
They were danced on in season.
They felt the touch of knees
At prayer time.
Over them were carried
The coffins of my ancestors.

But one day, by dint of fashion,
It was decided to lift them,
To make way for cement and linoleum.

But they are again on the mountainside,
They are exposed to the wind.
As a pathway to the well
New feet will tread them.

trans. author.

Moyra Donaldson

(1956-)

Poet and editor. Born in Newtownards, County Down. Educated at Queen's University, Belfast and at the University of Ulster, Coleraine. Published widely in magazines and anthologies, her work has been broadcast on BBC radio and television. She has won many awards for her poetry including being short-listed for *The Sunday Tribune*/Hennessy New Irish Writing Awards. Editor of three anthologies of work by writers' groups, she also writes for stage and screen. Her pamphlet, *Kissing Ghosts* appeared from Lapwing Publications in 1995. Themes of home and family, fidelities and betrayals of love and the bindings of myth and history permeate her poetry, making her one of Northern Ireland's most interesting emerging poets.

POETRY COLLECTION

Snakeskin Stilettos. (1998). Belfast, Lagan Press.

I DO NOT

I do not confess to anything – so when I speak
of the small dark spidery creature
skittling across the periphery of my vision –
it proves nothing.
Meaning is just an accident,
soon mopped up: those letters
were written by someone else,
and that suitcase under the bed
does not contain my heart.

I do not regret anything – so when the black dog
digs up the bones I have buried
beneath the brambles, deep in the wild woods –
I am not worried.
I have allowed no prophets
to enter my house, so bones can not
stand up, grow flesh and walk.
They cast no shadows
and I have nothing to look in the face.

I do not promise anything – so when I lie
down with you, close as a child,
intimate as a lover, tender as a mother –
it means nothing.
Love is just a trick of the light,
a misunderstanding.
No matter who you think I am,
when it matters most,
I will not be who you want.

Katie Donovan

(1962-)

Poet, essayist, editor and critic. She grew up on a farm in County Wexford. Educated at Trinity College and at the University of California at Berkeley, she taught English for a year in Hungary. She now works as a journalist for *The Irish Times*. In 1994 she edited with A. Norman Jeffares and Brendan Kennelly the anthology *Ireland's Women: Writing Past and Present*, in which an attempt was made to redress the imbalance created by the small representation of women in *The Field Day Anthology of Irish Writing*. She also edited an anthology of writings about Dublin, *Dublines*, with Brendan Kennelly in 1996. Published and broadcast in Ireland, Britain and the USA, her poetry is an exploration of myth and the physical world, bringing to Irish poetry a voice that speaks with courage and a refreshing openness.

POETRY COLLECTIONS

Watermelon Man. (1993). Newcastle upon Tyne, Bloodaxe Books.
Entering The Mare. (1997). Newcastle upon Tyne, Bloodaxe
    Books.

HIM

He washes through my senses –
a lovely dye –
tinting me rose and peach,
tanging me pineapple,
like edible chunks of sun.

He stops the traffic
as he brings
my flowering wrist
to the press
of his lips;
his big boot
alongside
my lifting toes.

I quicken:
a burst of birds
on a blue sky.
He takes me
like a river
takes a stone;
or like the arrow
he flourishes and fits,

and lets
fly

Mary Dorcey

(1950-)

Poet, short story writer and novelist. Born in Dublin, she has lived in France, Spain, England, America and Japan. Living now in Dublin, she is an important poet in contemporary Ireland. She is one of the first writers to acknowledge being lesbian and to express and address in her work Irish, lesbian and feminist concerns. In 1990 she won the Rooney Prize for Irish Literature for her book of stories *A Noise from the Woodshed* and was awarded an Arts Council Bursary in 1990 and 1995. Widely anthologised, her work has been translated into many languages and is taught in Irish Studies and Women's Studies courses at universities internationally. Compassion for the universality of sexual love marks her poetry. Her themes are lesbian love, nature, women's lives and sexual politics. Dorcey exhibits an acute sensitivity to language and the complexities of feminist and human nature. A research associate at Trinity College, Dublin, she has completed a fourth collection of poetry *Like Joy in Season, Like Sorrow*.

POETRY COLLECTIONS

Kindling. (1982). London, Onlywomen Press.
Moving into the Space Cleared by our Mothers. (1991).
    Galway, Salmon Publishing.
The River that Carries Me. (1995). Galway, Salmon Publishing.

EACH DAY OUR FIRST NIGHT

What a beautiful mother
I had –
forty years ago

when I was young
and in need of a mother.
Tall and graceful

dark haired
laughing.
What a fine mother I had

when I was young.
Now I climb the steps
to a cold house

and call out a word
that used to summon her.
An old woman comes to the door

gaunt-cheeked,
white-haired, feeble.
An old woman who

might be anybody's mother.
She fumbles with the locks
and smiles a greeting

as if the name spoken
belonged to her.
We go inside

and I make tea.
The routine questions
used to prompt her

fall idle.
She cannot remember
the day of the week,

the hour
nor the time of year.
Look at the grass,

I say
look at the leaves –
You tell me!

Autumn she answers
at last.
Her hands wind in her lap

Her eyes like a child's
full of shame.
Each day a little more

is lost of her.
Captured for an instant
then gone.

Everything that
made her particular
withering

like leaf from the tree:
her love of stories
and song, her wit.

The flesh on her bones.
What a beautiful mother
I had forty years ago

when I was young
and in need of a mother.
Proud, dark haired

laughing.
Now I descend the path
from a cold house.

An old woman
follows to the window.
An old woman who

might be anybody's mother.
She stands patiently
to wave me off

remembering
the stage directions,
of lifted hand

and longing gaze.
In this
experimental piece –

each day our first night –
she plays her part
with such command,

watching her
take a last bow
from the curtain –

I could swear
she had been
born for it!

Anna Marie Dowdican

(1969-)

Poet and painter. Born in Donegal, she studied Fine Art in Sligo for four years. An accomplished painter, she has had ten solo exhibitions and numerous group exhibitions nationwide. She has written many art critiques for local press and art publications. Her collection of poetry is a mélange of words and pictures which quietly reveal the restless and the tranquil in the human soul. A religious poet, she evokes echoes of Francis Thompson's "Hound of Heaven" in her work. Sligo Art Gallery has encouraged her in both her visual and poetic journey.

POETRY COLLECTION

Imagine. (1998). Black Battler Press, Sligo.

MINE BE

Mine be the strength of courage deep
Rushing swelling alive and free.

Mine be the faithfulness of the turning tide
The hidden depths of the green salt sea.

Mine be the silence of lonely hills
The face softened mists of grey shadow.

Mine be the brimming furnace of fires core.
The love of all and all and more

Mine be the life of veiled glances
The sighing winds and mystic trances
and
Mine be the life to live beyond poetic thought .....

Katherine Duffy

(1962-)

 Poet and fiction writer. Born in Dundalk, now lives in Dublin. She was educated at University College, Dublin where she studied English and Irish. She works as a librarian in Dublin. Her first poetry collection, *The Erratic Behaviour of Tides,* was published in 1998 and included work which won prizes in the National Women's Poetry competition and the Roscommon Abbey Writers competition. She has published fiction in English and Irish, has won Oireachtas awards and has been shortlisted for Hennessy Literary awards. Her novel for young adults *Splanctha!* was published in 1997 by Cló Iar Chonnachta. Her poetry is lyrical and charged with powerful imagery. Many poems are rooted in childhood memories.

POETRY COLLECTION

The Erratic Behaviour of Tides. (1998). Dublin, The Dedalus Press.

WEATHERWITCH

'... magic which has lost nearly all its power is apt
to become limited to weatherforecasting ...'
Edward A. Arnold, *The Folklore of Birds.*

The woman who tells the weather
speaks clearly, her voice true
to mountain and plain, to the unpredictable
ways of pressure and temperature.

Each day, we watch her cultivate
her garden of symbols: sculptured
clouds in white or grey, pennants
to flag the winds, yellow, childish suns.

We ask much of her; she must be
prophet, washing-line advisor, facilitator
of small talk ... Above all,
we want her to say it will be fine,

and when instead she speaks
spells and showers, drizzle, drought,
explicating cold-hearted charts,
we rail at her, denounce her power.

She looks unruffled, but who knows
what private blizzards of self-doubt
she endures. In another age, she
might have been formidable, a magician.

As it is, she commands the respect
of umbrellas. She holds traffic in thrall.
Apologising for snow, her voice is warm.
She wears an icy suit. She smiles.

Martina Evans

(1961-)

Poet and novelist. Born and educated in Cork. She trained as a radiographer at St. Vincent's Hospital, Dublin. In 1988 she moved to London where she received a degree in English and Philosophy. Her first novel was published by Heinemann in 1997. Her poetry has been published widely in magazines and newspapers in Ireland, Britain and the USA. Drawing on themes of colonisation, Irish childhood experience, love and motherhood, her poetry is in general written in the first person singular. Themes of sexual violence and cruelty to women and children are voiced in individual poems that read like dark fragments.

POETRY COLLECTIONS

The Iniscarra Bar and Cycle Rest. (1995). Herts,
    The Rockingham Press.
All Alcoholics Are Charmers. (1998). London, Anvil Press Poetry.

A QUIET MAN

i.m. Richard Cotter 1902-1988

He was a quiet man,
a secret man, who liked to be alone,
and he had ten children.

He couldn't bear to cut down his trees.

Every Christmas he defiantly brought in
the worst pine, with the scantiest branches,
and his family spent the whole Christmas
trying to cover it up.

Passionate about fires, inside or out,
he spent summer evenings tending crowds
of them in a field full of sunset.

He was a warm small-eyed man,
his hands were big,
his forever young pink-and-white skin
his crowning glory.

He could sing,
a fine dry note,
pucking out rebellious words.

He was a quiet man
though he'd kill for his dog.

He was a joker and a cod
and it was easy for him,
with all about him flapping their mouths
like multicoloured scarves in the wind.

He was a careful man,
though it could be construed as meanness:
'No fear he'd ever turn into an alcoholic!'

He liked Rum and Butter toffees, cherry brandy,
Sandyman's Port poured with a heavy hand,
tapping his broad fingers on the table.

His wife and children's mad grand sweeping
talk flew around the house like magic carpets.
He smiled and tapped and sipped.

He was a quiet man,
we could sit in a room,
the two of us, with no talk.

Maurice Farley

(1909-1999)

Poet. Maurice Farley is a pen name. She was Irish and lived in Dublin. She published poems in three anthologies: *Irish Poems of Today* edited by Geoffrey Taylor (1944), *Contemporary Irish Poetry* edited by Robert Greacen and Valentin Iremonger (1949), and *Poets Aloud Abu* Ink Sculptors, Cork (1988). She had work in many poetry magazines in Britain and Ireland including: *Poetry Ireland Review*, *The Salmon*, *Cyphers*, *Orbis*, *Chapman* and *The Irish Times*. Irish and European subjects are themes in her poems together with those of loss and memory.

POETRY COLLECTION *

Before the Cattle Raid and Other Poems. (1998). Belfast, Lapwing Press.

————

A HOUSE BY LOUGH CARRA

I have been anxious for my house in Mayo lately,
so many great houses have been burnt by the Republicans.
Mine is a Georgian house,
with four grey pillars and a flight of steps,
a lawn that the green lake laps.

There is a balcony where one may sit
and watch the evening darkening on the lake,
or pink of morning on the Partry hills.
How beautiful the day is on Lough Carra!
Under Muckloon
the heron dips his bill in cool green water,
little flags of spring wave on its meadowed edge.

I have not been there for many years now.
Is the lake water still green?
Do other boys row among the many islands
under Muckloon, where I rowed once with Maurice,
brother and friend, and now estranged?
No letters come from Ireland,
nothing between us but an empty house.

He should have been the heir, a country squire.
He used to revel in his grassy schemes,
a poet in stone and clay,
a dreamer who would not waken.
Moore Hall is dead and all its sister halls –
dreams that men hoped to make imperishable
in stone and marble, follies in granite,
flowers and terraces.
This was a feudal house, its day is gone.

Vale to Ireland, to the shattered dreams,
the inconclusive dwindling of a race
strong and imperious.
I have no heir and yet it lives in me.
It will be fitting if my ashes stand
over Lough Carra,
the dream commemorated by my hand
survive the house.
Mine was the harvest. Out of mists and trees,
lilacs and quarrels, ancestral memories
I plucked a pattern,
and the lake water rippled in my books.

Last night Moore Hall was burnt.
The flames lit up the sky,
startled the sleeping heron on his perch
under Muckloon,
and the invaders stood, watching it burn,
the four grey pillars and the flight of steps,
the balcony that looked upon the lake,
my great-grandfather's dream.

But the invaders too were men of dreams,
seeing the stables razed, the gardens tilled,
a hundred houses where one great house stood.

Pauline Fayne

(1954-)

 Poet. Born in Dublin, she left school aged fifteen. She lives in Tallaght and was a founder member of the Clothesline Writers' Group and The Clothesline Press, a community publishing group. Several of her poems have been anthologised in publications like *Four Urban Voices* – Raven Arts Press (1988), *Between the Circus and The Sewer* (1988) and in *Poets Aloud Abú* (1989). Fayne's collection *Journey* is a search for personal identity and awareness. She scrutinises her past in order to come to terms with it and its influence on her, both as a woman and as a poet.

POETRY COLLECTION

Journey. (1979). Dublin, Sheveck Press.

OPTIMISM

Tripped by misjudged moves
And alcohol sparked words
Into the three o'clock in the morning gutter
I watch the two-faced moon
Sidle across the brightening sky,
Await the inevitable sober dawn
While in the puddle beneath my feet
A sycamore leaf glistens
Frost crystallized,
A heelless shoe
Dances in the rain flow
And a child's lost marble
Winks its golden eye.

Janice Fitzpatrick-Simmons
(1954-)

Poet and teacher. Born in Boston and raised in Wellesley, Massachusetts and Rhode Island. She received a BA in Classics and in English Literature, from Franconia College, New Hampshire, USA in 1977 and an MA in English Literature in 1986, from the University of New Hampshire, Durham. She also studied at UCD and Queen's University, Belfast. She married the poet James Simmons in 1991. She taught at Queen's University, Belfast and the University of Ulster at Coleraine, and has given readings in England, America, Wales, Scotland, and Belgium. She was Assistant Director of the Robert Frost Place, where she set up the first exchange with Bernard Loughlin between the Robert Frost Place and the Tyrone Guthrie Centre, at Annaghmakerrig. Her poetry has appeared in many magazines and journals in Ireland, Britain and the USA and in *A Rage for Order*, an anthology of poetry of the Northern Ireland Troubles edited by Frank Ormsby (Blackstaff, 1992). Her pamphlet, *Leaving America* was published by Lapwing Publiations in 1992. Her themes are nature, fertility, love and the Irish landscape. She links contemporary Irish poetry and American poetry through her work at the Poets' House, County Donegal. At Poets' House she teaches the first BA programme in Creative Writing to be offered in Ireland, and has students from Ireland, Britain and the USA.

POETRY COLLECTIONS

Settler. (1995). Galway, Salmon Publishing.
Starting at Purgatory. (1999). County Clare, Salmon Publishing.

BALLROOM DANCING

I want you to look back
over the grey and purple sunrise
of a day in that other Donegal,
say on holiday with Tony and Bill,
camping near Greencastle's ruins,
walking to the Smugglers' Inn in the rain,
pissed, flirting with actresses, full of yourselves,
serious – a premonition of where
you've found yourself
in the lap of family under Muckish.

I want you to be always
kissing Eileen by the Foyle
in the wanton dark.
Stars pulse out the rhyme
of love and you are young
and singing sometimes in the Corinthian,
dancing there – ballroom dances
that I have learned like Latin verbs
to please my father.

'Here is the delicate turn,
the side step of the waltz,'
my father said. 'Turn your head,
come into the rhythm
and movement by looking back
over your shoulder.'

And I look back,
into the tentative eyes of a thirty-year-old,
a woman coming into herself,
bending over the water of the Gale.
One of your selves, the stranger,
scoops water in his hands

for his mistress, Mars and Venus
rise that evening low on the horizon,
dazzling those two caught there in time.

'And here is the trick,' my father said:
'To keep in step with your partner
dip and sweep a little forward
while you look back.'

Anne-Marie Fyfe

(1953-)

 Poet and teacher. Born in Cushendall, County Antrim she now lives in London where she is a Lecturer in English and Creative Writing at Richmond-upon-Thames College. She organises the Coffee-House series of readings at *The Troubadour* in Earls Court, runs the Richmond Poetry Society at Richmond Adult College and has published research on contemporary Irish women's writing in Image and Power (Longman, 1996). Since first appearing in *London Magazine* in 1993, her poems have been published in magazines and journals including: *Times Literary Supplement*, *The Independent*, *London Magazine*, *Poetry Ireland Review*, *The Rialto*, *Poetry London* and *Poetry Durham*. She has been a prizewinner in The Daily Telegraph Arvon International Poetry Competition (1998) and The Peterloo Poetry Competition (1999) and others. A pamphlet, *A House by the Sea*, published by Bellmead in 1995, was a short sequence of poems set against the Atlantic coastline. The poetry in her first collection combines that world with narratives of urban alienation and meditations on growth, love and loss. Tom Paulin has said of her poems [they] "have a lyric clarity, an ontological accuracy and unflinching vigilance that is both spiritual and revelatory."

POETRY COLLECTION
Late Crossing. (1999). Herts. Rockingham Press.

HALLSTAND

He would wear sandals with socks,
roll shirt sleeves
back beyond the elbow.

She wore crisp frocks,
blues and yellows; on the lapel
of her summer jacket, a silver
flower-basket brooch,
a gemstone for every bloom.

All summer on shore walks
I'd dawdle, lag behind,
collect limpets and whelks.
That year I was eleven,
changing schools; they'd talk
about my new uniform,
the price of convent shoes.

Odd evenings there'd be a quiet
heavy tone: silence as I'd catch up.

The rest of the summer froze
to a single family snapshot –
I'm standing by the hallstand
watching
as she leaves for hospital.

Each long evening,
bored on the slipway,
I'd tear the legs off crabs,
one by one, throw them back:
smash volleys on gable walls,
until the light would finally go.

The sandals stayed in the airing cupboard
all that summer. And the next.

Isobel Gamble

(1948-)

Poet, teacher, scriptwriter. Born in Moy, County Tyrone, she was educated at Dungannon Girls' High School and Queen's University, Belfast where she received a degree in Geography. A teacher for many years, she has had her poetry published in *Cyphers*, *Poetry Nottingham*, *Orbis* and other Irish and British magazines. She writes for children and has been scriptwriter for Radio Ulster's "One Potato, Two Potato." Her poems have been included in those broadcasts.

POETRY COLLECTION *

The Orchard. (1998). Belfast, Lapwing Publications.

LIKE MERCATOR

I grasped the bed knob –
Cold, smooth and spherical.
All the world I had in my hands
Though I did not know it then –
Hopes of an eternal spring.

Innocence was dropped by the pansy bed.
Mother tugged at my morals.
Like a caterpillar I crawled through the world
Up and down through the daffodil wood
Their trumpets tickling my legs.
I lay beside crocus sunsets
And marvelled at a merging into adulthood.
Like Mercator charting out my world
Mapping a new horizon, testing intuition
New answers, new questions
Puckered my fevered brow.

Sarah Gatley

(1955-)

 Poet and geologist. Born in Kent, England and educated at Leicester and Hull Universities, she undertook research at Trinity College, Dublin in 1981. On joining a creative workshop in Blackrock under the enthusiastic guidance of John Kelly, her writing became more prolific. Many of this group formed the core of South City Writers' Co-op in Stillorgan. Between 1989 and 1993 she participated in a number of workshops, including Trinity College's national workshops with Eavan Boland, Paul Durcan, Paula Meehan and Michael Longley. Her poetry has been published in *Poetry Ireland Review*, *Trinity Workshop Poets* and *Stet*. She has read at the Poets' Platform at the Cúirt International Festival of Literature in Galway.

POETRY COLLECTION *

Black Line On White. (1997). Belfast, Lapwing Publications.

WILD AFFAIR

I took him there in good faith,
and thought he was suffering with me
the inclemency of the weather;
Until on the fifth morning
when he rose, the rainswept vista
slanting his vision,
It dawned on me –
He was having an affair
with Achill;
and not even behind my back –
No he spoke of it openly then
and, unashamedly, told the islanders
that he loved the frenzy
of the wind, the whiplash of the rain,
the bursting of the rivers,
And that it must be the only way
to see her beauty,
feel the pull of her magic,
And they looked at him sideways –
and I did too.

Catherine Graham

(1964-)

Poet and teacher. Born in Hamilton, Ontario, Canada. She was educated at McMaster, Brook and Lancaster Universities and received an MA in Creative Writing from Lancaster in 1994. Her poetry has been published in various journals in Ireland, Britain and Canada and has been broadcast on BBC Radio Ulster. A selection of her work appeared in *Signals*, an anthology of poetry and prose (Abbey Press, 1997). Irish by descent and adoption, she lives and works in County Down. The poems in her collection *The Watch* are a moving account of a daughter's attempt to come to terms with the death of both parents. Honest and tender, they express a hopeful sense of renewal.

POETRY COLLECTION

The Watch. (1998). Newry and Belfast, Abbey Press.

THE WATCH

Six foot three, basking in tawny heat,
Sunk in his lounger, spring to September.

His face bakes like earth.
Chest hairs slice the sweat beads.

The black leather watch (he never forgot to unstrap)
Ticks beside his ghetto-blaster.

Cobalt eyes, silver thick hair, dentured smile,
Arms folded under the crest of his chest,

He poses for fall's final mould.

*

Later, after the black skid,
Spin and deep tip of the freshly polished blue Caddy;

After the crunch of his skull on the dashboard;
Even after the front page photo and headline:

My father's watch, still ticking,
Unzipped from the O.P.P.'s plastic.

No cracks, the glass smooth to touch.
Dry mud-flakes sprinkle like ashes

On to my opening hand.

Angela Greene

(1936-1997)

Poet and painter. Born in England, she lived from early childhood in Dublin. She was educated at Dominican College, Eccles Street and trained as a nurse at the Mater Hospital, Dublin. In 1988 she won the Patrick Kavanagh Award and in 1989 was short-listed for *The Sunday Tribune/ Hennessy Literary Award*. In 1987 she was a prizewinner in the Bloodaxe Books National Poetry Competition. Her poetry was published in Britain and Ireland, read on RTÉ Radio and BBC Radio Ulster and was performed in *Sunny Side Plucked* at the Project Arts Centre, Dublin. Her deeply lived experience as woman, daughter, wife, mother, poet and painter is reflected in quiet, well-crafted and moving poems. The lateness of her arrival to contemporary Irish poetry and the quiet way she received her well deserved recognition, makes her loss all the more poignant.

POETRY COLLECTION

Silence and the Blue Night. (1993). Galway, Salmon Publishing.

LETTING GO

The false security
of the simple
and the ordinary.

I lift the latch, push,
take several steps
across the bright linoleum

toward the dresser shouting,
'Kids, kids, I can hardly hear my ears,'
when I realise I am in a dream.

The fool in me
not wanting to accept change.
In that moment I had my children
as I still want them to be. Kilts
and knee-socks, short pants
and t-shirts. The soft splash
as milk
falls from the tray of the high chair.
I'm reaching back to them
from chat through chores
to play. What I didn't know then ...
That rowdy kitchen was a piece
of cake. I ruled the roost.

Now these young men and women
sprawl over so much space
they scare me. The world's
the oyster their minds
prise wide. They talk
inches above my head. Their
laughter and their language leap
beyond me.   Now

I am forced to look at time
in another way. Not
as so many grains of sand
flowing from glass belly
to glass belly, but how,
through the persistent gnawing
of years, I've weathered
as I watch them grow. And
how at last, as I let go
and slip behind them, I ease
my bones into the universe.

Pamela Greene

(1951-)

 Poet and lawyer. Born in Belfast, she was educated at Queen's University where she studied Spanish. A qualified solicitor, she currently practises law in Belfast. Her poem *voice in a bell-jar*, together with the title poem of her pamphlet, both appeared in the centenary issue of *Honest Ulsterman*. Her poetry has also been published by *Poetry Ireland Review*, *The Sunday Tribune*, *Full Moon* and *Figments*. She is a member of Ards Writers Group and has given readings throughout Ireland. She is currently working on a full collection.

POETRY COLLECTION *

Heartland. (1998). Belfast, Lapwing Publications.

VOICE IN A BELL-JAR

i have painted my beautiful girl
the colours of invisible
taught her to walk silent
through the world
as light through a prism

with barbed wire and thorn
i have braided her silken hair
in the moon's full light
placed a silver pentagram
at her milkycool brow

with odour of leafmould
i have disguised the
fragrance of her innocence
chained to her small wrist
a wolfhound with jaws of steel

but her flowering is stronger
than all my defences
around me and beyond me
she reaches for the sun
arms outstretched to embrace

would that the stone in my hand
were my heart made stone

Rene Greig

(1947-)

Poet and playwright. Born in Belfast and educated at the Girls' Model Grammar School. Studied music, voice and dance. In addition to writing poetry, she has written seven full-length plays. These have been performed throughout Ireland and at the Brighton Arts Festival. Her poetry has appeared in publications such as *Poetry Wales, Gown, Fortnight* and *Acorn* and has been broadcast on Radio 4. She has taught creative writing and theatre skills to children and community groups for several years. The poet Peter Pegnall has said of her poetry: "It can be jagged, startling, unruly as well as gracious and tender: here are the sights and sounds of a well-earned life, a Belfast Chronicle without cheap frills or slick cynicism."

POETRY COLLECTION

Through a Hedge Backwards. (1999). Bangor, County Down,
    Ha'Penny Press.

FILIGREE NETWORK

You understand how I feel when I see
hedgerows dusted with spider's webs
trapping dewdrops in a filigree network.
You'd package it, gift wrap it if you could.
Instead each New Year's Day, birthday,
you package the gift of a poem, that can't be bought.

When our third son was taken from us
we wrapped around each other in bed, shared tears.
We weathered the losing of two homes,
returned the keys, laughed and said
'It's only a roof with four walls,
a place to eat and lay our heads.'
Home is where the heart is, our children, you.

When you lost your job, were made redundant,
we picked up the pieces, cut our losses,
threw ourselves headlong into our shared love:
words, lines, poems, plays and us.

Wrenched apart outside Mullingar
when a forty-three foot truck
smacked and mangled our car.
A month of long lonely days and nights,
you in Tollymore and me in Mullingar.
We recovered, supported as broken bones mended.

I don't need a hedgerow dusted with spider's webs,
a filigree network, a packaged poem:
not with the delicate, priceless, real you.

Vona Groarke

(1964-)

Poet and curator. Born in Edgeworthstown, County Longford. Educated at Trinity College, Dublin and University College, Cork, she has worked in Britain, the USA and Norway. In 1992 she received an Arts Council Bursary and spent time writing at the Tyrone Guthrie Centre, Annaghmakerrig. She was joint winner of the Listowel Writers' Week Sonnet Competition and in 1994 she won the Hennessy Award for Poetry and *The Sunday Tribune* New Irish Writer of the Year Award. Her first collection, *Shale*, won the Brendan Behan Memorial Award in 1995 and in 1999 she won the Strokestown Poetry Competition. She has been writer-in-residence at NUI Maynooth in 1998 and NUI Galway in 1999. Clear, lyrical lines are characteristic of her poetry and she uses place and landscape to illuminate the narratives of herself as lover and family historian.

POETRY COLLECTIONS

Shale. (1994). Oldcastle, County Meath, The Gallery Press.
Other People's Houses. (1999). Oldcastle, County Meath,
    The Gallery Press.

HOUSE-BOUND

The blind holds it in check. As you let it down,
it tightens its grip on an evening otherwise unstirred.
What you see is a calculated hour which he is likely
to tie up in a darkened, half-dark upstairs room.

What he brings with him is another world. When,
with your loose fingers, you undo him, then its
refuse, fog, its chips and cigarettes rub off on you.
You can almost memorize it with your tongue.

He brings you messages. You take him at his word and
once a week allow him in. He thinks of missionaries,
the bond that never breaks. Not that it matters.
It's not company you're keeping, but your hand in.

The skein of darkness in his hands is another story.
He is tightening it all night, so that the stars you keep
initially at bay bear down and perforate your darker sky.
Inside of which you lie, and take it as it comes.

It should mean silence, but it never does. The unused
words thicken in your head, the room, your open door,
the road going out of town. Something like
'Good evening.' 'A great stretch.' 'How do you do?'

You think it is a double bind: on one hand, there's the dark
he lays you in; on the other, there's the chance that he might
mean the world to you. That one day, you may wake alone to
a shift of crumpled fields, a room released to light, an easy life.

Kerry Hardie

(1951-)

Poet. Born in Singapore she grew up in County Down. She lives in County Kilkenny. Widely published in magazines and literary journals in Ireland and in Britain, she has twice won *The Works'* Women's National Poetry Prize and received prizes and commendations in the Observer Arvon, Cardiff International and Peterloo poetry competitions. A number of her poems appeared in her pamphlet *In Sickness* from Honest Ulsterman Publications in 1995. Joint winner of the 1995 Hennessy Award for Poetry and winner of the 1996 National Poetry Competition, her poems reflect her deep sense of place and her relationship to suffering born out of devastating illness. Her debut collection received the acclaim it richly deserved.

POETRY COLLECTION

A Furious Place. (1996). Oldcastle, County Meath, Gallery Press.

SHE REPLIES TO CARMEL'S LETTER

It was a mild Christmas, the small fine rain kept washing over,
so I coated myself in plastics,
walked further than I could manage.
– *Leave me now* – I'd say, and when they had tramped ahead
I'd sit myself down on a stone or the side of a high grass ditch,
or anywhere – like a duck in a puddle –
I'd rest a bit then I would muddle around
the winding boreens that crawled the headland.

Sometimes, water-proofed and not caring,
I'd sit in the road which was really a stream-bed,
being and seeing, from low, where the hare sees –
try it sometime, sitting in mud and in wetness,
the world rising hummocky round you,
the sudden grass on the skyline,
the fence-post, with the earth run from under it,
swinging like a hanged man,

till you would want to praise
the ease of low wet things, the song of them,
like a child's low drone,
and praising you'd watch how the water flowing the track
is clear, so you might not see it
but for the cross-hatched place where it runs on a scatter of grit,
the flat, swelled place where it slides itself over a stone.
So now, when you write how you labour to strip off the layers,
that there might not, under them, be anything at all,

I remember that time, and I wish you had sat there, with me,
your skin fever-hot, the lovely wet coldness of winter mud and grass
on your red, uncovered hands, knowing the point is the layers,
the flesh on the bones, the patterns that the bones push
upwards onto the flesh.
So, you will see how it is with me,
and that sometimes even sickness is generous
and takes you by the hand and sits you
beside things you would otherwise have passed over –

Anne Le Marquand Hartigan

(1937-)

Poet, painter, playwright, performer. Her mother was Irish, from County Louth, and her father was from the Channel Islands. She studied fine art at the University of Reading, England, specialising in painting, and has lived in Ireland since 1962. She has won awards for her poetry, plays and batik. A founder member of the Women's Studies Forum at UCD and the Women's Artists Action Group, she has also served on the Executive of the Irish Writers' Union. In 1982 and in 1989 she had plays performed at the Dublin Theatre Festival. Her awards include Listowel Writers' Week Open Poetry Award, 1978; Yeats International Summer School Scholarship, 1978; Poetry Athlone Award, 1980; The Mobil Oil Prize for Playwriting, Ireland, 1995. She has received many bursaries including one from The Irish Writers' Union to Hungary (1994) Writers' Exchange and the Stewart Parker Trust Bursary (1990). Themes in her poetry include love, birth and death. She celebrates women, giving them voice through history, myth, religion and nature.

POETRY COLLECTIONS

Long Tongue. (1982). Dublin, Beaver Row Press.
Return Single. (1986). Dublin, Beaver Row Press.
Now is a Moveable Feast. (1991). Galway, Salmon Publishing.
Immortal Sins. (1994). Galway, Salmon Publishing.

EPISTLES IN WINTER

Estuary

Through you I touch many continents
many childhoods
times past of blood and love, cold
countries thaw
and the hot do not burn up, but
warm on

We make children in the night with
no darkness
in our mingling spittle words brood
the lip-lap
of language makes channels for flow
for gush
for the swift mind – the touch imperative.
We're cousins of bone and steel,
yet we melt

Saline

clash of brine and flesh;
bog-wine
dung song peat tone, ice of salt
cracks a note. Staccato of teeth and bite.
The edge of black/white. Tongue of difference
spear bud-acid spring ache
the lick of it. Hard spit.

River

Bend your head and I will baptise you
so you can surface into the watermoon
there are prayers arrayed, chants and candles
melodies of blessings sing in the bird's throat
supplications of incense call our introits
they spiral into the ether breath
the moon catches and the sun consumes

eat my body.

Bend your head and with oil I will anoint you,
genuflect, kneel together in this solemn novena
take nine first Fridays to ensure a pathway
standing as the Baptist up to his knees in the flow
holding a shell to plunge, dip the waters.
The thirst drove us here, total immersion, risking
belief without doubting where enchantment burns,

drink my blood.

Anne Haverty

(1959-)

Poet, novelist, biographer. Born in County Tipperary and educated at Trinity College, Dublin, she has lived in Paris and London and now lives in Dublin. Her biography of Constance Markievicz was published in 1988 and her acclaimed novel *One Day as a Tiger* (Chatto 1997) won the Rooney Prize and was short-listed for the Whitbread First Novel Award. Her first collection of poetry, *The Beauty of the Moon,* was a Poetry Book Society Recommendation and brings together new poems and poems which have been previously published in Ireland and England. Together with quietly intimate poems Haverty also addresses the disillusionment associated with *fin de siècle*. The poet Derek Mahon calls her "a singing voice for our dejected age."

POETRY COLLECTION

The Beauty of the Moon. (1999). London, Chatto and Windus.

LADIES WAITING ROOM, THURLES STATION

Cool as a milk churn, bare as a mountain field,
A smoulder of sods in the grate, that winter scent –
Before I came to know her, this room did; the chair,
The butter-coloured walls, the grey wainscotting. Her
Coty powder perfumed its air for an hour –
A voice complains outside; a delay at the Junction –
And Blackie neighs in the station-yard as my ghostly
Grandfather gives him the nod. Now they've gone.

She was a girl in a red coat going back to Dublin.
Some stranger maybe combing her hair half-saw
That precious face in the mirror and remarked
The train was late. My mother, I imagine, agreed;
Politely, absently, as she often did ... Briefly, I am she.
But what else she said, or really thought, is lost to me.

Rita Ann Higgins
(1955-)

 Poet, playwright. Born in Galway, her formal education ceased when she was a teenager. Self-educated later when recovering from tuberculosis. In 1982, encouraged by the members of the Galway Writers' workshop, she began to write poetry. In the early 1990s two plays, *Face Licker Come Home* and *God-of-the-Hatch Man*, were produced by Galway's Punchbag Theatre. She received bursaries in 1986, 1989, 1992 and 1993 from the Arts Council, has broadcast and travelled extensively giving readings and workshops, and in 1989 won the Peadar O'Donnell Award. She was writer-in-residence in University College, Galway in 1995 and was elected a member of Aosdána in 1996. She was Galway County writer-in-residence in 1987 and Offaly County Council writer-in-residence in Tullamore in 1999. An explicit, sardonic and witty social commentator, her poetry releases the angry, often sad voice in her head. Her poetic response to the Galway and Ireland in which she grew up continues to fascinate her many readers at home and abroad.

POETRY COLLECTIONS

Goddess on the Mervue Bus. (1986). Galway, Salmon Publishing.
Witch in the Bushes. (1988). Galway, Salmon Publishing.
Goddess and Witch. (1990). Galway, Salmon Publishing.
Philomena's Revenge. (1992). Galway, Salmon Publishing.
Higher Purchase. (1996). County Clare, Salmon Publishing.
Sunny Side Plucked: Selected Poems. (1996). Newcastle upon Tyne, Bloodaxe.

THE WEATHER BEATERS

The bitter snap is over
a few bones told them.
The two of them leg it
through the green
a hundred steps more or less
and the cure will be in hand.

The winter was too long
this is the first bright day
and true to form
pep came back to step
it out across the Prairie
the only open space in Castle Park.

They are not as old as they look
these weather beaters
karate-expert-weather-beaters
they box it and kick it
with their falling-off toes
they shout while they do it
one says the snow is an animal
a pig dog with warts the other says.

This bright day has given them hope
anti-freeze-cider-hope
they're walking faster now
they leg it across the green
faster than they did in ages.

The flea-infested couch they got
as a so-called Christmas present
can go to blazes
they think this in unison
with their bachelor brains.

Today they stretch their bones
their funny bones
everything is funny today
they say hello to two kids lighting a fire
the kids say fuck off and die
the weather beaters laugh and laugh.

Máire Holmes

(1952-)

Poet, playwright, fiction-writer, dramatist. Born in Dublin and educated at the Dominican College, Eccles St., and at University College, Galway where she is at present outreach writer. Published widely in English and Irish, her work is also on the Leaving Certificate course. Her short story *Smile For Mammy* has been awarded the Hennessy Prize and her plays have been performed at the National Theatre and at Taibhdhearc na Gallimhe. She has broadcast for RTÉ and BBC and is a regular contributor to Raidio Na Gaeltachta. Two of her researched programmes made in the USA were screened by TG4. She is a Artistic Director of The Connemara Theatre Company and is shareholder of the National Theatre. Her poetry has been published in *The Salmon, Writing in the West, Cyphers* and many Irish and English publications. Her first choral piece PAX will be performed at the opening night of the new theatre in Armagh. Sharply poignant, her poetry is filled with striking, natural imagery.

POETRY COLLECTION

Dúrún. (1988). Baile Átha Cliath, Coiscéim.

IARFHLAITH

Three boats sail home
towards the evening of your third month.
On the oceans of the world
aged ships sail with
indifference,
but your young blue eyes focus
knowing no fear.
You cannot hear unfathomable forces
and yet know nothing of dangerous depths.

Towards the evening
of your third month
the swans on the Corrib
ignore your youth,
scaling the Claddagh basin
indifferent
to passing dogs
who boast four legs
are better than two.
At three months
your fresh blue eyes focus
and your feet dance
to a future that will spread wings
over this century.
As I hold you,
I see you walking away,
going towards exploration
beyond now
Iarfhlaith, you will learn nothing of
indifference
from me,
for I will care
deeper than the ocean
and farther than any swan can ever fly.

Tess Hurson

(1955)

Poet. Born in Annaghbeg on the Tyrone/Armagh border and educated at Trinity College, Dublin, Queen's University, Belfast and York University, Toronto. Her doctoral thesis was on the novels of Flann O'Brien. She now works as Student Support Officer and Assistant to the Director at Queen's University, Armagh. She has published and broadcast widely on literature, local history, community arts, culture and social issues. Her poetry has been published in *Fortnight, Belfast News Letter, Honest Ulsterman* and *The Linnet* and has been broadcast on BBC Radio Ulster. Her themes include philosophy, politics and popular culture, together with themes of love and a disabled child's entrapment.

POETRY COLLECTION

Vivarium. (1997). Belfast, Lagan Press.

IN THE SNOWSTORM

for Eva

Halfway out the Hilltown Road she senses
Tilted on its random axis, the world
Outside the car implode with noiseless snow.
They would be left on back hall ledges;
Smudged, blindsided, made in China, plastic domes,
Tipped for amusement by nosy children,
The sugar snow birls briefly upwards
Then silts down in some vague innuendo;
A story that never gets imagined.
Within the hemisphere, immobilised,
She asks forever her speechless how.
But for some magic dedicated man
Who arcs infinity and springs her out
To mingle with the Hilltown hares
To lie where ducking valentinos dive
To climb through blue Kilimanjaro,
Snow spinning in her mouth like casual words.

Biddy Jenkinson

(1949-)

Mórfhile agus sár scríbhneoir í. Ainm cleite is ea Biddy Jenkinson. Tá a cuid filíochta ar shiollabas na scoile le fada an lá. Tá roinnt drámaí foilsithe aici. Craoladh iad ar RTÉ faoi stiúir Sheáin Uí Bhriain. Cuiread *Aisling Ghéar*, dráma leí, ar ardán i mBéal Feiriste, Eanáir 1999. Bhuaigh drámaí léi, nár léiríodh fós, duaiseanna ó Amharclann na Péacóige agus Amharclann de hÍde i gcomórtaisí an Oireachtais. Foilsíodh a gearrscéalta i *gComhar*, *Oghma*, *Feasta*, agus san nuachtán *Lá*. Tá sé i gceist ag *Coiscéim* cnúasach gearrscéalta leí, *Lúidín an Phíobaire*, a fhoilsiú go luath. Bhíodh colún cócaireachta san nuachtán *Lá* aici ó 1997 go 1998. Is duine de na mórfhilí is cáiliúla í. Tá clú idirnáisiúnnta ar a cuid filíochta. Bronnadh duaiseanna uirthi in Éirinn is i Meiriceá; duais an Oireachtais don leabhar *Amhras Neimhe*, 1997, duais ón gComhairle Ealaíona don leabhar *Uiscí Beatha*, 1992, duais an Mhaolánaigh do ghearrscéal, 1997, agus duais filíochta ón bhFondúireacht Ghael-Mheiriceánach, 1997.

CNUASAIGH FILÍOCHTA

Baisteadh Gintlí (1986). Baile Átha Cliath, Coiscéim.
Uiscí Beatha. (1988). Baile Átha Cliath, Coiscéim.
Dán na hUidhre. (1991). Baile Átha Cliath, Coiscéim.
Amhras Neimhe. (1997). Baile Átha Cliath, Coiscéim.

MAIDIR LEIS NA DÁNTA SA LEABHAR SEO

Ní heol dom cé thóg an balla sléibhe seo
atá á atógáil agam im intinn ... duine ...
Ní heol dom cé chuir na lusanna ... duine ...
B'é Loren Eiseley a d'aimsigh mo bhlaosc cinn dom
    thall i Meiriceá.
Ní rabhas riamh in Alabama.
Níl bó ná buaile ná baile ar leith agam
is beirim liom siúicre an bhóthair mar leasú dáin.
Níl ginealach ar leith agam
ná tír
ná dílseacht
ná inscne
ná leanbh
ná leannán.
Tada ní liom.
Liomsa an Uile
ar mhaithe le dán.

Is táim á rá le duine ar bith a chumfadh cuid na filíochta
a dhéanfadh mionléarscáil de dhúthaigh na samhlaíochta,
a dhéanfadh daonáireamh
a d'ainmneodh Tobar an Fheasa
a chuirfeadh stápla in eireaball an bhradáin.

Is táim á rá leis ar fhaitíos go gcreidfeadh sé m'fhírinní
a shiúlann ar chosa bréige
ar fhaitíos go dtabharfadh sé taitneamh d'im seo mo
chuiginne
gan beann aige ar an mbreac ealaíonta sa bhláthach.

118

EN RÉFÉRENCE AUX POEMES DE CE LIVRE

J'ignore qui a érigé ce mur dans la montagne
que je reconstruis en pensée ..... quelqu'un
J'ignore qui a planté ces herbes ...... quelqu'un
C'est Loren Eiseley qui m'a trouvé ce crane en Amerique
Je n'ai jamais visité l'Alabama
Je n'ai ni vache ni pâ turage
Je n'ai pas de toit fixe
et j'emporte la poudre routière pour fertiliser mes poèmes
J'e n'ai pas d'ancêtres
pas de pays
pas de loyauté
pas de sexe
pas d'enfant
pas d'amant
Je n'ai rien
Tout est mien
pour écrire un poème

Je l'annonce à qui veut rationner la poésie
tracer le pays de l'Imagination
Recenser
Nommer la Source du Savoir
et ferrer la queue du saumon

Et je le dis de crainte qu'il puisse
croire mes vérites perchées sur des jambes artificielles
de crainte qu'il puisse decider aimer ce beurre de ma baratte
sans payer attention à la truite farceuse dans le lait.

trans. Mireille Harnett.

Maeve Kelly

(1930-)

 Poet, novelist and short story writer. Born in County Clare and educated in Dundalk, County Louth. She trained as a nurse in London and did post-graduate work in Oxford. She lives in Limerick where she has been involved with women's groups and social organisations for many years. Winner of a Hennessy Award for her short fiction in 1972 and better known as a novelist and short-story writer, she has written and published poetry for many years and gives workshops and lectures on the work of Irish women writers including Kate O'Brien. Her poetry collection reflects the isolation of the lives of rural women and issues surrounding women as victims in Irish patriarchal society.

POETRY COLLECTION

Resolution. (1986). Belfast, Blackstaff Press.

PRIMO LEVI'S PRAYER

If I was God
I would spit at Kuhn's prayer
who knelt on his bunk
his beret on his head
praising his god
because he had not been chosen.

When the copper rain came down
the blood on the paving stone
ran to meet it.
They flowed together,
and rushed to the hungry one who waited.

The sea will open its mouth
to swallow their endeavour,
and when the burnt cities have decayed
and all the rivers have dried,
only the fools will say,
we will remember them forever.

Rita Kelly

(1953-)

Poet and short story writer. Born in County Galway and educated there, she writes in English and Irish. Winner of the Merriman Poetry Award in 1975, the Seán Ó Riordáin Memorial Prize for Poetry in 1980 and the recipient of an Arts Council Bursary in 1985. Her first book, *Dialann sa Díseart*, was written with her husband, the late Eoghan Ó Tuairisc, and is a record of her life with him. She lived in New York for five years, taught creative writing and has given readings in Ireland, Europe and the USA; her poetry has been published and anthologised widely. She has been writer-in-residence for County Laois and has worked with writers in Portlaoise Prison. Translated into German, Dutch and Italian, her spare style has no sentimentality and she is direct and honest about cruelty experienced by women.

POETRY COLLECTIONS

Dialann sa Díseart. (1981). Baile Átha Cliath, Coiscéim
     (with Eoghan Ó Tuairisc).
An Bealach Éadóigh. (1984). Baile Átha Cliath, Coiscéim.
Fare Well: Beir Beannacht. (1990). Dublin, Attic Press.

BEIR BEANNACHT

D'éalaigh tú thar chiumhais na maidine,
ní nach ionadh
bhí an t-éalú ionchollaithe i do theacht.
Fanaim
ag comhaireamh na mbáisteachaí thar an fhuinneog,
sileann an t-am.

Ritheann sé liom go bhfuil duine éigin
ag an doras, téim:
asclán bláthanna, aghaidh choitianta, fear
in éadaí dubha –
sea, is mise, domsa, duitse –
spréann na feileastraim in a gclaimhte,
lasracha gorma ina bhaclainn aige.
Nach rídheas an mhaise duit
an lá a chur trí thine.

Iris – teachtaire na nDéithe
cuireadh go *Díodó* í san annallód
leis an aon fhuascailt amháin
d'éinne atá ag lúbarnaíl ar an mbreocharn
agus *Aeinéas* imithe leis chun a dhán
a líonadh.

Anois
níl fágtha ach leid an mhiotais:
na feileastraim sínte ar an mbord
agus faoin mbord sínte
faic.

Tá do chailleadh gan chorp.
Ní féidir an fhoilmhe a chur faoin bhfód.

FARE WELL

You crept away over the edge of morning,
no great wonder really,
the going was embodied in your coming.
I remain
counting the rains which fall across the window,
time spills.

It occurs to me that
there is somebody at the door, I go:
a bouquet of flowers, a common face,
a man in dark clothes –
yes, that's me, for me? For you.
Irises, spread, spears,
blue flames across his arms.
How lovely of you
to set my day ablaze.

Iris – messenger of the gods,
she was sent to *Dido* long ago
with death, the only relief
for a body writhing on a pyre
and *Aeneas* gone off with himself
to fulfil his fate and keep word.

Now
there is only left a hint of myth:
irises stretched on a bare table
and stretched under the table
nothing.

Your loss is without a corpse.
There is no burying an emptiness.

trans. author

Anne Kennedy

(1935-1998)

Poet, photographer, teacher and broadcaster. Born in Los Angeles and educated at Stanford and the University of California at Berkeley. Lived in Laurel Canyon in the 1960s among artists, musicians and writers before moving to Orcas Island in the San Juans, north of Seattle. Living in Galway since 1977, she worked as a photographer before joining the Galway Writers' Workshop in 1986. Her poetry has appeared in many journals and anthologies in Ireland and the USA. Her experiences of life as daughter, mother, friend and lover shine through poems rooted in the USA and Ireland. Her compassionate vision broadened the field of contemporary Irish poetry written by women. Her jazz research undertaken with Rex Stewart has been acquired by The Smithsonian Institute in the USA for their Duke Ellington archive. In June 1997 she participated in The Socrates programme in Brittany, France, a cultural exchange between Parma, Odense, L'orient and Galway. She prepared an exhibition of photographic black and white prints which toured the libraries of the four participating cities. A selection of her poems has been translated into Breton and French. She was working on a volume of memoirs, and a third poetry collection, when in late 1998 she lost her long battle against cancer.

POETRY COLLECTIONS
Buck Mountain Poems. (1989). Galway, Salmon Publishing.
The Dog Kubla Dreams My Life. (1994). Galway, Salmon
Publishing.

WITH ONE CONTINUOUS BREATH

I have stepped out
onto that same patch of grass
a thousand times,
it is my Heraclitean stream.
You, jingling your car keys,
me, wearing the low-cut lilac dress,
eager for the Italian meal,
unsure, always unsure.
Only your hieratic gestures:
tipping the head waiter,
calling him by name,
assure me you too are uncertain.

Up on the hill our house
dissolving in a sea of lights,
under chaparral, granite decomposing
our oranges slightly sour,
more lemons than we could ever use,
the jacaranda;
life in such profusion.

Again and again I step
out of the car your father gave us,
too posh
too grand for newly marrieds.
The grass springs sere under my lilac sandals,
petal sleeves, beehive, eyes absurdly kohled.
With one continuous breath
I absorb the pungent night air,
never dreaming
that from all our years together
this moment only will sting.

Jessie Lendennie

(1946-)

Poet and publisher. Born in Arkansas, USA and educated at King's College, London. She moved to Galway in 1981 and was a founder member of the Galway Writing Workshop in October of that year. She was a founding editor of *The Salmon* magazine (1982) and co-founder of Salmon Publishing, 1985. Since 1986 she has run the press at its Director. She was Chairperson of the Poetry Co-Operative which was set up in 1983 to promote the work of local poets and bring international poets to the West of Ireland. She was co-organiser of the first Galway International Poetry Festival in 1984 and a founding member, in 1985, of the organising committee of Cuirt, the International Literature Festival in Galway. Her poetry has been anthologised in *Irish Poetry Now: Other Voices* and *Unveiling Treasures: The Attic Guide To The Published Works of Irish Women Literary Writers*, among others. In 1990 she was nominated for a Bank of Ireland Arts Award for service to the arts in Ireland. Her prose-poem *Daughter* demonstrates her ability to write powerfully about the darkness experienced in childhood and its effects, in turn, which direct the way life and the imagination are shaped by these shadows. Lendennie is also the author of *The Salmon Guide to Poetry Publishing in Ireland* and *The Salmon Guide to Creative Writing in Ireland*.

POETRY COLLECTION

Daughter. (1988). Galway, Salmon Publishing / Washington USA, The Signpost Press Inc.

BETWEEN US

It is that Irish mid-August
so common now;
wind holding the slanting rain
in place for hours
then sudden sunlight
as I watch your departing train
moving along the bay.

I see how the sun shines
on this sleek silver water
a mirror of gulls
I wade in seaweed
deep as an uncut field
and remember
you at King's Cross Station
riding the escalator backwards
and my son saying
      'I know you miss him when he's gone'.

As if I never knew better
as if I never knew where we would be
these few years later
parting on a day when
a sudden wind
puts the sunlight
between us.

Catherine Phil MacCarthy

(1954-)

Poet and drama teacher. Born in Crecora, County Limerick. She was educated at University College, Cork and later studied drama at Trinity College, Dublin and in London. She lives in Dublin where she teaches drama and creative writing and publishes her poetry regularly in magazines and newspapers. Joint winner of the Poetry Ireland/Co-operation North *Sense of Place* competition in 1991, a selection of her work was published under the title *How High the Moon*. She won the National Women's Poetry Competition in 1990 and was a prizewinner in the 1992 Patrick Kavanagh Awards. RTÉ Radio 1 has broadcast her poems and they have appeared in anthologies and in special Irish issues of USA literary magazines such as *The Seneca Review* and *Irish Studies Review*. She was editor of Poetry Ireland Review Nos. 57-60. The landscape of an Irish country childhood permeates her poems, sharpened by the hidden secrets and cruelties of a society determined to oppress its women. In turn subversive and powerfully erotic, her work has won the praise of Eavan Boland who wrote that her poems have "the sort of music that reaches outwards and into the memory."

POETRY COLLECTIONS

This Hour of the Tide. (1994). Galway, Salmon Publishing.
The Blue Globe. (1998). Belfast, The Blackstaff Press.

SAND GODDESS

On the beach at Smerwick
a figure scooped out of sand –
breast, navel, genitals,
decorated with spirals of shells,
that stove light like
breakers on the shore.

Eyes, nose, mouth, stones.
Seaweed green hair.
There for the spoiling as if
she were the same
as any other castle.
What man and woman divined

a goddess from their play
leaving soundless joy
in the air about her?
Has she no name? Could it be
Duibhne of the black hair
come to restore us to history?

Children take turns lying
in the valley of her thighs
as if birthed from her womb,
and ferried all at once
in the boat of her knees,
they row the stream over stones,

jump out to snuggle at her side,
ask if it's possible to get inside her,
failing that, gingerly lift
the shell of her nipple,
take an eye out of her head
leaving her matter-of-factly blind,

their touching at first
awed by the reality
that a woman is a body
they have never been this close to,
and finally that a woman is a body
even they can dismantle.

Carmen Mac Garrigle

(1965-)

Poet. Born in London, she was raised in Northern Ireland. She lived in County Donegal for some years and now lives in Gwynedd, North Wales. Nominated for a Hennessy Award in 1997, she was also Best Donegal Poet at the Allingham Festival that year. She received scholarships to The Poets' House in 1992, the Kerry International Summer School (K.I.S.S) in 1995 and 1997 and was a British National Poetry Competition winner in 1995. She has read her poetry widely throughout Ireland and has participated in *Writing Across Borders*, an 18-month series of writing workshops with *The Hammer Writers*, Belfast. These were moderated by, among others: Joan Newmann, Simon Armitage and Jessie Lendennie. Also a scriptwriter she worked with *The Errigal Writers* and playwright Marie Hannigan in 1997. The strength of her poetry is her ability to transform the ordinary.

POETRY COLLECTION *

Journey From The Dead Room. (1998). Belfast, Lapwing Publications.

ADAMANT

In the beginning was the word.
You dangled apples from ceilings,
held my hands behind my back.
And I, the fool, dived in to take
the first bite
We played Finders, Keepers
until I lost the rules of the game.

Sometimes, in occasional madness,
I'd float before you in Opium
and chiffon negligee.
You preferred to watch Panoramic views
on Norwegian Cod-Fishing.

In middle years, in terminal sadness
I lay in bed
played Snap in my head,
turned tablet into stone,
mastered the art of serenity,
until I became invisible.

In the end, when you got custody
of my hand-spun throws,
television set and sanity,
I knew it was time to leave.

I call myself Eve,
check into a hotel
in my assumed name,
refuse all offers of Apple Strudel
from adamant older men,
fish for compliments from younger game,
always have the last word.

Eilish Martin

(1945-)

Poet and teacher. Born in Belfast she was educated at St. Dominic's High School and later at Trinity College, Dublin. She taught in London and Belfast. She became a member of the Word of Mouth collective in 1994 and started to send her work out for publication. She has given readings at the Old Museum Arts Centre, Belfast, The Belfast Festival, the Sligo Arts Festival and at the Kerry International Summer School (K.I.S.S.). Short-listed for a Hennessy Award in 1955, she was a prizewinner also in the National Women's Poetry competition. Her poetry has appeared in Honest Ulsterman, New Irish Writing, *The Sunday Tribune* and in Women's Work. Poems have been broadcast by BBC TV Northern Ireland, BBC Radio Ulster and RTÉ Radio 1. Ruth Carr, associate editor of *Honest Ulsterman*, has said of her poetry: [Martin] "renders defining moments of loss, of illumination, or of quiet reflections in language that is at once compressed and expansive, sensuous and philosophical."

POETRY COLLECTION
slitting the tongues of jackdaws. (1999). Donegal, Summer
　　Palace Press.

DAYS OF ABSTINENCE

I have painted a woman bending over a sink,
running water through a collander of herring.
A woman who has sons and daughters.
Certain devices hint at intimacy

– her apron, an old shirt, its sleeves
wrapped around her waist
– a boning knife on the draining board, its handle
wound with cord for better grip.

And oh, the lustre of the woman's bare arms.
I have put a girl by this woman's side,
balancing on tiptoe, steadying herself against the sink

– a girl whose head is full of the figurine
on the mantelpiece in the front room, a porcelain
dancer with eyes fired to an all-over white
intent on the door, listening for her music
so she can begin.

But there, where the girl imagines the delph dancer, there
is where narrative steps outside its fixing agents
– the mediums of beeswax, of albumen
of gum from the acacia tree –

leaving all kinds of plots to thicken in rooms
where everything,
even the utility furniture in chintz covers,
is waiting to begin,

and I become absorbed with the rust of blood
crusting under fingernails
the brilliance of fishes' scales gloving a woman's hands

the soluble quality of oil in ether

suggesting the robust grace
of two women roughed-in,
inclining towards one another
on days of abstinence.

Orla Martin

(1969-)

Poet and teacher. Born in Dublin, she grew up in Tipperary. Educated at St. Patrick's College, Maynooth where she studied French and Anthropology and University College, Cork. Worked as a modern languages teacher in Ireland and Europe for some years. In 1996 she worked as Literature Officer for Tigh Fhilí in Cork. She has given readings at literary and Arts festivals in Cork, Limerick and Dublin. Executive Director of Clé, The Irish Book Publishers Association, she now lives in Dublin. The poet Gabriel Fitzmaurice writing of her work, has said that whether she writes about human relationships or female sexuality, hers is the voice of a brave and independent mind.

POETRY COLLECTION

The Trek from Venus. (1996). Cork, bradshaw books.

AUNTS MATTERED

Aunts mattered: they had histories, businesses.
Families spoke of aunts differently – boxed them in,
a gift of mannerism, truth and speculation,
each visit preceded by a summary
of what they might say, had done, could be, in my head.

The facts were simple: aunts had no husbands,
shared a house, fought often, twice refused the home,
hurt feelings all round – their voices breaking glass.
A fine film of perfumed dust fell
every time they offered cheeks I had to kiss.

Not that we were ever intimate: cruel as familiars are,
their relatives would never take the bait.
When names of former beaus were dropped
they stayed, at a respectable distance,
remote as years abroad,
bound in tea-chests on the top floor.
Aunts always had more room than they needed.

Moved to hired care they started being grateful,
smiled more often, changed tactics,
watched our faces and grew smaller.
I was glad I'd seen them, at large,
proud and vigilant, pouring tea
in china cups, reading richer sorts of fortune.

Caitlín Maude

(1941-1982)

Poet, dramatist, singer and actress. Born in Casla in the Connemara Gaeltacht, she was raised in Cill Bhriocáin, Rosmuc where her mother taught. Educated locally, she graduated in 1962 from University College, Galway with a degree in English, Irish, French and Maths. Multi-talented, she was renowned for her role in Máire Ní Ghráda's *An Triail* when it was staged in 1964. A *sean-nós* singer, Gael-Linn, the Irish recording company, issued an album of her singing and poetry in 1975. The quality and purity of Caitlín's voice and her mastery of traditional songs sung in the centuries-old style produced something both unique and truly moving. She was deeply committed to social justice, to worthy causes, the Irish language and her native Gaeltacht. Her poems reflect her passion for life and her idealism. A free spirit, she wrote poetry from an early age and was recognised as one of the best of modern Irish poets. She read widely in Ireland and initiated the annual exchange of Scottish Gàidhlig and Irish poets in 1971. She explores many themes in her poetry, not least her illness which held her captive in the final year of her life. One poem, *Géibheann*, in which she compares herself to a caged wild animal, its strength, beauty and zest stunted prematurely, was – ironically and tragically – written in the mid 1960s and not, as is sometimes thought, during her illness. Her untimely death in 1982 was a tragedy not alone for her husband Cathal Ó Luain, her young son Caomhán, and her friends, but a tragedy for Ireland, for all Celts and for Irish poetry and traditions.

POETRY COLLECTIONS

Caitlín Maude, Dánta. Ciarán Ó Coigligh a chuir in eagar.
(1984). Baile Átha Cliath, Coiscéim.
Caitlín Maude. (1988). Baile Átha Cliath, Coiscéim.
Caitlín Maude: file. (1985). Italy, edizioni dal sud /
Baile Átha Cliath, Coiscéim.

LIOBAR

Mura bhfuil mé
go mór ag dul amú
stiall é.
Sclamha gadhair
go tréan ar a imeall

nó aríst ar ais
b'fhéidir gurb é
rian an tsiosúir
atá air. Gearrtha mín,
amach ón dúid
slíochta, 'nós an phéarla.

Tá sé ráite gur déanadh
cuid mhaith dochtúireachta air.
(Idir mise is tusa is cuma).
Is leor gur léir
nach bhfuil ann ach píosa de rud eicínt
níos mó ná é féin.

Níos mó!
I bhfad níos mó!
I bhfad Éireann níos mó!

Le tréiscint na haoise
tháinig malairt datha air.

Mo thrua!
Níor aithnigh a mhianach féin é
Is é ag brú gaoil orthu 'feadh an ama.

Dochtúirí, muis, a mharaigh é,
Lucht ceirde is pleanála.
Stuaim, a mhic ó,
a chuir sna brilleogaí liatha é.

Ach dar m'fhocal!
Más marbh féin é

Tá sé glan.

Glan, a deirim, glan.
Chomh glan leis an gcriostal.

Bricfeasta an tsagairt,
ní bheadh náire ort é a leagan air.

Nó

An Chroch Chéasta orainn!
An Chomaoineach Bheannaithe.

TATTER

Unless I be
greatly mistaken
It is a strip –
Several dog-bites
violent on its edge –

or again
It may be
scissors' cut –
Cut fine
from the base,
Sleek like pearl.

It is said it was
much doctored
('tween you and me it's equal).
Suffice to say
'tis but a piece of something
greater than itself.

Greater!
Much greater!
By Ireland's length much greater!
With age's fading
its colour changed.

Alas!
Its own kind did not ken it
And it insisting on kinship ceaselessly.

Doctors, indeed, killed it –
experts and planners.
Skill, boy,
That put it with the fairies.

But, 'pon my word,
Though it be dead

It is clean!

Clean, I say, clean.
As clean as crystal.

The priest's breakfast
you wouldn't be ashamed to place upon it

Or
– the Cross of Christ on us! –
The Blessed Host.

trans. Rosangela Barone.

Joan McBreen

(1944-)

Poet and teacher. Born and grew up in Sligo. Educated at the Ursuline Convent, Sligo; later trained as a primary teacher at the Froebel College of Education, Sion Hill, Dublin. She taught for many years in Dublin, Limerick, Ballaghaderreen, County Roscommon and Tuam, County Galway where she now lives. She received an MA degree in Women's Studies from UCD in 1997. She is influenced by the life and poetry of W.B. Yeats, Patrick Kavanagh and Louis MacNeice. Meeting Eavan Boland in 1986 was a pivotal moment in her life as a poet. Boland's early interest and support was central to her development, as was the support she found in the Galway Writers' Workshop, of which she is still a member. Published widely nationally and internationally, her poetry has been translated into Italian and French and regularly appears in anthologies, poetry magazines, journals and newspapers in Ireland and abroad. A frequent broadcaster on RTÉ Radio 1, she gives workshops and readings throughout Ireland. Childhood, love, loss and the Irish landscape are all features that mark her poetry.

POETRY COLLECTIONS

The Wind Beyond The Wall. (1990). Oregon, Story Line Press.
A Walled Garden in Moylough. (1995). Galway, Salmon
    Publishing / Oregon, Story Line Press.

THE MOUNTAIN ASH

If you can imagine it
fully grown, red berries
in clusters on every branch,
and if you understand
my desire to tend it
always in my own place,
you will know why I carried
it here as a sapling,
uncovered the roots from plastic,
exposed them to the cold air.

This sheltered garden
will never resemble
its wild hills nor the soil
deceive as black earth
of the mountain, yet
I can be seduced into believing
my mountain ash
will live, and day after day
draw me to the window,
allow me rise with certainty.

I carry my washing in and out
in great armfuls,
bring a necessary stake
to my mountain ash when it struggles
against the harsher winds.
Blind with sleet, on days I cannot
see my face in the mirror
it comforts me as neither child
nor lover could. I planted it.
Without me it will die.

Kathleen McCracken

(1960-)

Poet. Born in Dundalk, Ontario, Canada, she studied Irish literature and creative writing at York University and the University of Toronto. She came to live in Ireland in 1989 and now lives in Belfast. She teaches English literature at the University of Ulster, Jordanstown, and gives readings and poetry workshops throughout Northern Ireland. Her poetry has appeared in *Honest Ulsterman*, *Poetry Ireland* and *Fortnight* and she works in writers-in-schools schemes for Northern Ireland. Published widely in Canada in magazines such as *Canadian Women Studies* and *The Malahat Review*, she is a poet who brings the landscapes of Canada and Ireland into her poems, making connections between psyche and place.

POETRY COLLECTIONS

Reflections. (1978). Canada, Fiddlehead Press.
Into Celebration. (1980). Canada, Coach House Press.
The Constancy of Objects. (1988). Canada, Penumbra Press.
Blue Light Bay and College. (1991). Canada, Penumbra Press.

GREEN POOL WITH LIGHTNING

in memoriam Shirley Valerie McCracken Marshall

Our faces ring the circumference
of a bluestone well, making their
circle around her –
porthole, iris, sunspot,
the halo of a candle.

She is all our mothers,
we are every one
of her children.
She is not drowning.
She is not waving, either.

This is not a cancer ward –
it is a green pool
and she is swimming, her laugh
the radiant collision
of lightning into water

or a trap-line
with every mechanism sprung
wide open, the ghost of a chance
escaping into conifers,
the cathedral silence of Sarawak wood.

Our watching is a wreath
of sweetgrass. It is burning
and we are letting her leave,
a winter mink into the snowscape,
spring salmon arcing back over
bales of air, into water.

Linda McDermott

(1962-)

Poet. Born in Derry, she moved to live in Killybegs, County Donegal in 1971, where she later co-founded The Killybegs Writers Group. She worked for a short time for the local newspaper *The Donegal Democrat*, and she encouraged many Irish writers to the area to give readings and workshops. She has a BA in Philosophy and English Literature. Her poetry is published in many Irish literary magazines; it explores ironies of power, politics and gender issues.

POETRY COLLECTION *

The Catch Poems. (1997). Lapwing Publications.

THE RIVER

I was beside the river
Its motion soft on white rock

I was the giver inside the flow
Above and under churning core

I was the weeper too
Learning my route and its pain

(There is passion in the salmon's silent refrain
there is grace in her returning)

l was branch dipped low
In the ebb of season break

I was for an unknown sake
Treasoned by illusion

Fingered waves of confusion
Licked her murmerless drop
And sang

Where is my Irish mother
Where are her faults and twists
Where is her chuckle
And wailing lament
Where are the stories of youth spent
And life spending
Where the willow is bending
Kissing the dance
Where motion is soft on white rock
Where heels kick and songs lick the moment
Where movement is in God's hands
Where life is sacred
And death more sacred still

She is the kiss of weed on my neck
Turning Orchid in tomorrow's eye
She is the river
        the dance
        the kiss
    the salmon's swim
    the rock
            and the core
She is history's mistress
And the church's whore
She is white as virgin
She is life ripe and giver
She is the willow
kissing the dance of the river.

Medbh McGuckian

(1950-)

Poet. Born in Belfast, she was educated at Queen's University. She taught English for several years before becoming its first woman poet-in-residence. She won Britain's National Poetry Competition in 1979 and published two pamphlets, *Single Ladies* and *Portrait of Joanna*, before her first collection appeared from Oxford University Press in 1982. Her prizes include: The Cheltenham Award, The Alice Hunt Bartlett Prize, The Rooney Prize and the Bass Ireland Award for Literature, and her 1991 collection *Marconi's Cottage* was shortlisted for *The Irish Times*/Aer Lingus Irish Literature Prize for Poetry. Her career as a poet has richly earned her many honours in Ireland and abroad, including in 1998 being the recipient of the Ireland Funds' Literary Award. She has been Visiting Fellow at the University of California at Berkeley and travels extensively to readings and conferences internationally. Her imagery and sensuous use of language challenge and mesmerise her readers, and continue to fascinate. Unusual syntax, shifts in tense, voices within voices in the poetry have had her critics agree with her own statement that her language has a logic of its own, "which may be the opposite of men's." She teaches, writes and raises a family in Belfast, bringing all the complex strands of her female experience to her poetry. She is considered one of Ireland's leading contemporary poets.

POETRY COLLECTIONS

The Flower Master. (1982). Oxford and New York, Oxford
University Press.
The Flower Master and Other Poems. (1993). Oldcastle, County
Meath, Gallery Press.

Venus and the Rain. (1984). Oxford and New York, Oxford University *Press.*

Venus and the Rain. (1995). revised ed. Oldcastle, County Meath, Gallery Press.

On Ballycastle Beach. (1988). Oxford and Winston – Salem, N.C., Oxford University Press and Wake Forest University Press.

Two Women, Two Shores, Poems by Medbh McGuckian and Nuala Archer. (1989). Galway and Baltimore MD, Salmon Publishing and New Poets Series.

Marconi's Cottage (1991). Oldcastle, County Meath, Gallery Press.

Captain Lavender. (1995). Oldcastle, County Meath, Gallery Press.

Selected Poems. (1997). Oldcastle, County Meath, Gallery Press.

Shelmalier. (1998). Oldcastle, County Meath, Gallery Press.

THE PRESENCE OF HER ABSENCE

When she squeezes tears softly
to manipulate the beyond,
I kiss at the unimproved road
and the spilt religion of her year-round
continuously dry iris-fold,
fluted along its whole length.

Its runoff moisture is a beautiful
weapon point at the window opening
of an old church, a wave pulse
in a lit up, fishbone lined tunnel
under a smooth sea, where fish
have designed their own eyes.

She repeats a word in an almost
touching way, and the words
that fly about the house all day
pull her backwards and forwards
in their daily pucker at the bird-
bone of her husk-confined ear.

As each page is read it is destroyed
forever, but I promise the next thing
soon, the pain-powder, the conscious
moon, the all-important lantern
with its over-powering warmth,
savage as her moment of waking:

a Sunday anyway, and the coming
and going part of the me
she is always with. Because we talk,
nothing meaningful gets said,
except that something has to happen
which it never does

to the mound of clothing on the floor
of the room, the taken-for-granted
slimmest of gold bands.
I would give France an island
or two, this unique morning,
to be outside her sleep, not now.

Ethna McKiernan

(1944-)

Poet. Born in New York and moved to Minnesota, via Ireland. She was educated in the USA and received a Bachelor of Science degree from the University of Minnesota and is a recipient of a Minnesota State Arts Board grant. Her poetry has appeared in magazines in Ireland and the USA, and Fireweed Press included her in the volume *Unlacing: Ten Irish American Women Poets*. Her collection *Caravan* was a nominee for the Minnesota Book Awards. Anthologies in which her work has appeared include *Eclectic Literary Forum – The 1999 Minnesota Poetry Calendar*, *The North Stone Review* and *The Next Parish Over: A Collection of Irish-American Fiction and Poetry* (New Rivers Press, Minneapolis). A first generation Irish-American, her poems reflect her life as a woman in both cultures and she expresses a profound sensitivity to the dilemma of the emigrant. Many dark voices are heard in her work, none more compelling than her own. She manages the firm of Irish Books and Media in Minneapolis where she now lives.

POETRY COLLECTION

Caravan. (1989). Dublin, The Dedalus Press / Minneapolis, Midwest Villages and Voices.

DRIVING THE COAST ROAD TO DINGLE
for John Sweetser 1919-1998

The light was thinning. Dusk fell
in soft haphazard clumps on the sheep,
the hills, the long streak of sea
below, the boys sprawled across
the back seat, their smell of wet wool,
of child-musk and sleep.

Ahead, two horse-trailers took the curves
slow and their brake-lights deepened
on-off, on-off, a red glow. Who
could hear me singing on this road
above the sea, who could hear
the leaps and dives my heart made
on-off, on-off, as I drove?

We headed west into dark
toward the harbour-town
whose name repeated in my brain
like rain sweeping now
across the windshield. The Volvo
skimmed hedge-rows to the left
and my hands gripped the steering wheel
a few times before the boys woke up.

At that moment
stars began to push
their white necks through
the shawled sky above.
I knew then there was no
inch of earth, no
other world than this
I loved.

Kathleen McPhilemy

(1947-)

Poet. Born in Belfast where she was educated. Attended University in Leicester, followed by study in London, Manchester and Edinburgh where she was awarded a Ph.D. for her work on the contemporary long poem in Britain and the USA (1980). Her first poem was published by James Simmons in *The Honest Ulsterman* in 1968. Child-rearing interrupted her writing career but she started again when she joined a poetry group in Camden, London. She has lived in Oxfordshire for the last ten years and her latest book was published with grant aid from the Greater London Arts. Her poetry has appeared in many journals and magazines including: *Verse*, *Fortnight*, *Oxford Poetry*, *Rhinoceros*, *Acumen* and *Rialto*. The author of four pamphlets published between 1983 and 1993, her poetry is both personal and political, holding firmly to the two ideas of poet as witness and the power of the human imagination. Although she has lived almost all her adult life in Britain, she thinks of herself as an Irish poet, or more specifically, a poet made in the North of Ireland.

POETRY COLLECTIONS

Witness to Magic. (1990). London, Hearing Eye.
A Tented Peace. (1995). London, Katabasis Press.

CHRISTMAS 1989

Wrong to say despaired of; the century flames
dangerous as a firework's last surprise
and beautiful; light falls on our faces
from hand-held torches, from all the carried candles.

Good news comes and comes by television
a corner opens from our lighted rooms
to a place of darkness that is full of lights
and every light a name we had forgotten.

A fitful flame that flickers as it flares
but lights a space too huge for irony;
no matter if it all should come to tears
we've seen what's marvellous, beyond our narrowing dreams.

Liz McSkeane

(1956-)

Poet and teacher. Born in Glasgow of Irish-Scottish parents. She has lived in Dublin since 1981 where she has been a teacher and has worked in educational radio and broadcasting for RTÉ. A former co-chairperson of the Dublin Writers' Workshop (1981-1991), she edited two issues of their magazine *Acorn* and has published her poetry in many magazines.

POETRY COLLECTION *

In Flight. (1995). Belfast, Lapwing Publications.

COLD TURKEY

The other day so unobtrusively
I barely noticed, anger left and since
the agitation's gone this vacancy
is bothering me. Living's less intense
when rage burns out, there's too much life to fill.
I miss the turbulence, the highs and lows
that make you feel alive. Just being still
takes practice. Deprives you of a purpose.
Like red meat, anger over-stimulates
the senses. It creates an appetite
for spice and anything more delicate
– like peace, for instance – tastes too bland, too slight
to sharpen up perceptions that can't see
the point of getting used to being free.

Máighréad Medbh

(1959-)

Poet, rap/rock performer. Born in Limerick where she was educated. She has lived in Dublin and Belfast. A witty and uninhibited commentator on Church and State, her poetry charts her life from birth through childhood and adolescence, through to motherhood and life in a patriarchal world. Irreverent and aggressive, her rhythms, taken from rock, reggae and rap, startle and shock the reader. A member of the Dublin Writers' Workshop, her poetry has been published in several anthologies including *The Virago Book of Wicked Verse, Ireland's Women Writings – Past and Present, I Wouldn't Thank You for a Valentine* (Viking) and others. In 1998 she won Dublin's first Poetry Slam, gaining the title 'Bard of Temple Bar'. Her second collection *Tenant* is a narrative sequence, following the fictional O'Sullivan family through the traumatic famine years, 1845 to 1849.

POETRY COLLECTION

The Making of a Pagan. (1990). Belfast, The Blackstaff Press.
Tenant. (1999). County Clare, Salmon Publishing.

MY DAY
March 1845

i sit up in our bed of straw and listen to the birds
we're a wild bunch of bodies all the same
– straw over, straw under –
mammy shuddered when i wondered
if we're kindred to the animals with no souls

she crossed herself and cathal frowned and i stuttered
to explain –
we're in the same byre, walk the same miry floor,
we eat together, sleep together in our clothes
the connors children run out naked
not just summer, winter too
even them that's in the bigger places
under gowns and mirrored faces –
well i never finished out my say
cathal went 'you better not' and i was on my own again
thinking things that turn me into something wrong

there's she's up and by the fire like she always seems to be
like an israelite waiting for the word
the boys are on their straw, daddy's in the loft
they're asleep but it's never silent here –
hoo and cluck and grunt and chew and the sounds that
blow in to us
people passing, children crying on the road
with the slit of window light and the brightening of the turf
i can see that she's looking at me straight
she gives her sunday of a smile
– you know i'd see it dark or bright –
and i make out what she's holding in her lap
it's my only good bodice that i stitched up late last night
so i'd cut a dash like any at the wake
'rena, girl,' she says, 'you're a fine young woman now
i was thinking this must be your birthdate'

she says i needn't wish for more than this
the birds gone mad with spring
potatoes in the pit
myself pink and healthy and fourteen
i get water from the well and look closely in the pail
splash my face with my reflection, comb my hair
i'll be watching for the man who'll know i understand
who'll whisk me like a story far away
a poet or professor or a travelling prince
i'll be pretty, simply waiting for my day

Paula Meehan

(1955-)

Poet and playwright. Born in Dublin she grew up in the north inner city. She was educated at Trinity College, Dublin and Eastern Washington University USA. She is considered one of Ireland's leading poets. Her awards include two Arts Council Bursaries in Literature (1987 and 1990) and the Martin Toonder Award for Literature (1996). She was elected a member of Aosdána in 1996. Two of her plays were commissioned by TEAM Theatre in Education company for primary school children, *Kirkle* (1995) and *The Voyage* (1997). Her play *Mrs Sweeney*, premiered by Rough Magic in May 1999, was published by New Island Books in April 1999. *Cell*, a new play, premiered in Dublin in 1999. She received The Butler Award for Poetry from the Irish American Cultural Institute in 1998. Passion, love, betrayal, recovery and the confusion of self-definition mark her poetry. Her voice, always alert to the public world, is evenly pitched against the private.

POETRY COLLECTIONS

Return and No Blame. (1984). Dublin, Beaver Row Press.
Reading the Sky. (1986). Dublin, Beaver Row Press.
The Man Who Was Marked by Winter. (1991). Dublin, The Gallery Press / USA Eastern Washington University Press. (1994).
Pillow Talk. (1994). Dublin, The Gallery Press.
Mysteries of the Home. (1996). Bloodaxe Books, Newcastle upon Tyne.
Selected Poems. (1999). Carcanet Press, Manchester.

THE TRAPPED WOMAN OF THE INTERNET

She turns to me or any other watcher
her freaked almond eyes: I imagine she says
rescue me, rescue me. And the only
rescue I can mount is to shift website
from Asiatic Babe Cutie Triple XXX Sexpot.
     Yet much as I want I cannot leave her
rest. She bothers me all the mundane livelong day.
I carry her to the edges of my own lonely
room, and in the coldest hour of this winter's night
I lay her down upon a fragrant cot

of dried meadow grasses, strewing herbs,
and off her thin and pallid face
I sponge the thick and viscid stuff;
     and at this point before the fire, I have to curb
such useless gesture towards an empty space
where no one can be saved, or loved enough

to save ourselves from our own virtual childhoods,
to puzzle ourselves free from those enchanted woods.

Máire Mhac an tSaoi

(1922-)

Poet and scholar. She was born in Dublin, the eldest of three children. She was educated in Alexandra School, Dublin; Scoil Ghobnait, Dún Chaoin, County Kerry and Beaufort High School, Rathfarnham. Her many distinguished degrees include a BA in Celtic Studies and Modern Languages (1941), and an MA in Classical Modern Irish (1945) from University College, Dublin. She studied at the *Institut des Hautes Études en Sorbonne*, University of Paris. From 1941-1944 she studied Law at King's Inns, Dublin and was called to the Irish Bar in 1944. She entered the Dublin Ministry of Foreign Affairs in 1947 and served in Paris, Madrid and Dublin. A member of the Irish Delegation to the General Assembly of the United Nations, 1957-60, she was also appointed Permanent Representative of Ireland to the Council of Europe, Strasbourg in 1961. She married Dr. Conor Cruise O'Brien in 1962 and accompanied him during his periods of residence in Africa, London and the United States. Writing principally in Irish, she was one of the team that compiled the *English-Irish Dictionary*, published in Dublin in 1959, edited by Professor Tomás De Bhaldraithe. She has edited a substantial body of work from Classical Irish and is an authority on traditional Bardic Poetry. Her pure motifs earn her the reputation of being a modern international poet of the highest calibre. She was editor of *Poetry Ireland Review* Nos. 31-33 and her poetry has been on the school syllabus for many years. Awarded a D. Lit. Celt. honoris causa by the National University of Ireland in 1992, she was also the winner of the O'Shaughnessy Poetry Award of the Irish American Cultural Institute, 1988. She is considered a significant poet and scholar in the Ireland of our time. Her poem *Shoa* is included in *The Great Book of Ireland* where it is illustrated by a survivor of the Nazi camps who signed his work with his tattooed number.

POETRY COLLECTIONS

Margadh na Saoire. (1956). Baile Átha Cliath, Sairséal agus Dill.
A Heart Full of Thought. Translations from Classical Gaelic Poetry. (1959). Baile Átha Cliath, Dolmen Press.
Codladh an Ghaisígh. (1973). Baile Átha Cliath, Sairséal agus Dill.
An Galar Dúbhach. (1980). Baile Átha Cliath, Sairséal agus Dill.
An Cion go dTí Seo. (1988). Baile Átha Cliath, Sairséal Ó Marcaigh.
Trasládáil. (1997). Belfast, Lagan Press.
Shoa, agus Dánta Eile. Forthcoming.

SHOA

*(Ar fheiscint dhealbh chuimhneachán íobairt
na tine i Vienna dhom – Samhain 1988)*

An seanóir Giúdach ar a cheithre cnámha,
Ualach sneachta ar a ghuailne,
Cianta an rogha ina ghnúis –
'Mar seo,' adeir an t-íomhá miotail,
'Do sciúr mo chine "leacacha na sráide"
I *Wien* na hOstaire, leathchéad bliain ó shoin –
É sin, agus ar lean é –
Ní náire feacadh i láthair Dé ---

Ach sibhse, na meacain scoiltithe,
Bhur gcoilgsheasamh ar bhur "gcuaillí arda",
Níl agaibh teicheadh ón aithis:
Ársa na mBeann crapadh go hísle glún,
Beatha na n-éag insa láib,
Ar a chosa deiridh don mbrútach!'

SHOA

*(On seeing the memorial of the Holocaust
in Vienna – November 1988)*

The old Jew on his hands and knees,
A weight of snow on his shoulders,
Ages of election in his face –
'Thus' says the metal image,
'My people scoured "the flagstones of the street"
In Vienna of Austria, fifty years ago –
That, and what followed –
It is no shame to crouch in the face of God ---

But you, the forked root vegetables,
Bolt upright on your "high stilts",
You shall not escape defilement:
The Ancient of the High Places stunted as low as the knee,
Eternal Life in the mud,
The brute on his hind legs!'

*Note: The phrases in inverted commas are taken from
a folk poem on Christ's passion.*

trans. author.

Áine Miller

(1944-)

Poet and short story writer. Born in Cork and was educated at University College, Cork. Lived in London with her family for some years, later returned to Dublin where she began to write stories and poetry and attend creative writing workshops. She has won many prizes for her work and is included in several anthologies of poetry, including the Wexford publication *Women's Work*. Winner of a Hennessy Literary Award in 1987, her first collection appeared in *Six For Gold*, published by *The Works*, December 1980. She won the 1992 Patrick Kavanagh Award, The Listowel Writers' Week Poetry Prize and a prize in the Scottish International Poetry Awards. She received her M. Phil (Creative Writing) degree from the University of Dublin, Trinity College in 1998. Her poetry, clear and accessible, draws its themes from autobiography, her relationships in family and in the small details of the domestic. Her tone is quiet and restrained, yet demonstrates a gift for intimating menace below the surface of the lived life.

POETRY COLLECTION

Goldfish in a Baby Bath. (1994). Galway, Salmon Publishing.

THE SILENCE CLOTH

Mother brought it from *The North*,
an inward land way off the point

in Cork, a land of once and *used to be*
grown to the stuff of silence. This cloth,

red dark chenille and bobble-fringed,
rough-textured as the cat's tongue,

clogged the sideboard drawer
so fully, the lock teeth didn't meet,

opened spontaneously. We fancied sighs
from that winy mouth, heard nothing

but the faint knocking of worms
in the wood, the shimmy of prisms.

When we were left to mind the house,
we unleashed the cloth, hung it

as a curtain in the archway.
Hamlet's speeches ballooned our sails.

We rode on rhetoric. With bare bodkins
silenced the pratings of old men.

Spread across the dully shining heart
of the French mahogany table

at Christmas, it served its true purpose.
Under the skin of damask and Irish lace

it lay like an unhealed bruise,
while we pretended to be ordinary,

swopped Christmas cracker jokes,
affecting not to see how cut glass

indented silence, and the little stabs
of fork tongues left holes slow to heal.

Lynda Moran

(1948-)

Poet, playwright, and short story writer. Born in the Midlands, her work has been published widely in Ireland and the USA. She has broadcast on RTÉ Radio 1 and 2, and in 1983 won the National Radio Award. She took part in the 1984 National Writers' Workshop, moderated by Eavan Boland. The themes of her poetry include suicide and loneliness. She reaches out from internal landscapes and uses an intense short line. Creating a sometimes chilling atmosphere, Moran's poetry is challenging and highly individual.

POETRY COLLECTION

The Truth About Lucy. (1985). Dublin, Beaver Row Press.

FAMINE SONG

Nothing pleases me more
than her half-heard song
from a worn half-door.
Clipped unconscious it sounds
familiar, strange.
Maybe a remnant
from some other childhood store.

Small the walled fields;
barren spaces where yesterday's acreage
harvests cunning April snow.
Lord Travelyn, did you know
the 'idle' Irish loved stories?
Hungry stones sprout acrospires;
funny how memories make shadows grow.

You remember the famine?
Of course. And the roads
going nowhere; how clever
to make murder suicide.
Look, the half-door is now open;
she notes corpsing celebration.
Stones record the day you died.

Sinéad Morrissey

(1972-)

Poet and teacher. Born in Portadown. She was educated in Belfast and at Trinity College, Dublin where she received a degree in English and German. She has worked as a teacher in Northern Germany, spent some time in Japan and New Zealand, and now lives in County Antrim. A prizewinner for five years in the Irish Schools' Creative Writing Awards, she became the youngest recipient of the Patrick Kavanagh Poetry Award in 1990. Her poetry has appeared in many journals and literary reviews and she is represented by her powerful poem *Ciara* in *Ireland's Women – Writings Past and Present*, (1994). Morrissey acknowledges a debt of gratitude to the Welsh poet R. S. Thomas, indicating that he inspires her "because he is absolutely faithful to his own poetic concerns, regardless of .... changing literary fashions." There are a number of poems in her first collection dealing with angels and the implications of religious faith.

POETRY COLLECTION

There was Fire in Vancouver. (1996). Manchester, Carcanet Press.

———

ON WAITAKERE DAM
for Charles Brown

You wanted to up-end the boat
& set it on the lake we lived by
because no-one would know.
It was lavish with silverfish & looked
defeated, humped on its secret
like a hand. There was nowhere to go to

but the magnet of the middle-lake
where a vapour sat wide as Australia –
as sovereign, as separate, as intimate
with daylight, as ignorant
of clocks & raincoats & boats.
It threw a soft, unwatchable shimmer

we would not be human in.
You dismantled a sky
as you tipped the boat over;
the nest of a possum was robbed.
The hull settled outside-in
as you inverted the universe.

We bobbed in the reeds. The trees
lay down their crowns beneath us –
an underwater canvas
of spectacular women. Above us
the crowds of their branches were cold.
Black swans were nesting in the nesting place,

trees reared to the rim of vision –
we slid on to the centre. At night,
with no lights for miles, the lake
would glitter with the Southern Cross.
It smiled at us
with a million silver teeth.

We'd heard it roar with rain
& watched it coughing eels
over the dam's brim,
too water-sore to keep them
any longer. They fell flinching themselves
into s's or n's.

& now we sat stilled in a boat
in the centre, under
the lake's shroud, & the listening
was for the car of the caretaker –
weaving down from the Nihotupu Dam
with Handel or Bach on the radio.

Iris Murdoch

(1919-1999)

 Novelist, poet and philosopher. Born in Dublin, she grew up in England and was educated at Oxford and Cambridge. A Fellow of Saint Anne's College, Oxford, she taught philosophy for many years. Murdoch made her debut as a writer in 1954 with her novel *Under the Net*. Among the honours and awards she received were the James Tate Black Memorial Prize, the Whitbread Literary Award and the Booker Prize. In 1987 she was appointed Dame Commander, Order of the British Empire. Her twenty-seven novels include the Booker Prize-winning *The Sea, The Sea* (1978), *The Philosopher's Pupil* (1990), *The Green Knight* (1994) and her last novel, *Jackson's Dilemma*. (1995). She also wrote several works of philosophy, criticism and drama. Her only published collection of poetry, *A Year of Birds*, (1978) was illustrated by Reynolds Stone. She married the scholar and critic John Bayley in 1956. By the 1970s her reputation was international and her influence great. In recent years this most intellectual of novelists was silenced by Alzheimers. She died in Oxford in early February 1999. Of her inclusion in this book, John Bayley has said: "Iris would have been delighted to be included as an Irish woman poet."

POETRY COLLECTION

A Year of Birds. (1978). London, Chatto and Windus.

MOTORIST AND DEAD BIRD

He felt or thought he felt the crack,
Saw in his mirror the bird-blotted road,
Cursed the compulsion of going back
To find it glossy, without blood, quite dead.
Pinned to the tarmac in a quick fight,
The wings embattled, the affronted eyes,
A sort of sudden trophy, whose near-flight
Still gibbers in the trees.
Swift memory adept at chance
Advantages implants the sting.
He recalls his wife and how she would have wept
Now, who wept once at such a thing.
She is not dead, not she, nor yet bereft,
But living happily with someone else.
She loved animals. After he left
They said it was a blessing they were childless.
No rancour; she describes her kids in Christmas letters.
He lifts the bird by a long wing-tip up.
Not to feel warm just-fled life is better.
Lays it in the ditch as if that could help,
Where leaves are tender: now abrupts the pains
Of vain remorse; and soon his pale
Headlights will scan the hawthorn lanes
That lead to the obscure hotel
Where he is waited for.
                    He will not tell
His little friend this creepy tale.
Her tears, his spite,
Will end in sleepy night.

Lizz Murphy

(1950-)

Poet and publicist. Born in Belfast, where she grew up. Educated at the Girls Model Grammar School and Fane Street Secondary School in Belfast. Later she attended Smith Hill Girls High School in Australia, but left formal education early. She now lives in the village of Binalong in New South Wales. Writing for over twenty years, she won the National Anutech Poetry Prize in 1994 and was awarded the 1998 Creative Arts Fellowship for Literature. Widely published in magazines and journals. She has published four anthologies including *Wee Girls: Women Writing from an Irish Perspective* with Spinifex Press in 1996. This includes fiction, poetry and autobiography by women writing from an Irish perspective in Australia, Ireland, England, America, Canada and New Zealand. Together with writing full-time, she is involved in creative writing work-shops, freelance editing and publicity.

POETRY COLLECTIONS

Do Fish Get Seasick. (1994). Australia, Polonius Press.
Pearls and Bullets. (1997). Australia, Island Press.

COLD ENOUGH FOR SNOW

It's cold enough for snow we used to say and it does
I bend my head as far back as I can Face a swarming
sky white swirl on white a pause and it sheds itself again
quickly quickly yet so softly a shower of whispers
It's not the first time I've seen snow fall on an Australian
landscape yet it seems new inconsistent with what I have
come to believe in

Two magpies take a close look bomb one another and
head for the trees burrow in There are no branches bared
like bones here although one eucalyptus leaf has fallen
is now iced on to my shoe I feel the cold wet bite through
leather I think of people without shoes children without
feet What if this trick of nature is really a side effect of
governments at work what if I have walked around in
eaten nuclear fallout Another pause a silent explosion
then feathers fall tufts of fairy floss hit the ground instant
meltdown I go back inside continue faxing media with
news of 'jellyfish babies' * as peace activists arrive at
the Mururoa Atoll

There is no real evidence of the weather gone haywire
only a scarified sky settling in for the evening
If I hadn't looked up just then I wouldn't have known it
had happened at all and now I can't pretend anything else

* From *Daughters of the Pacific* by Zohl dé Istar (Spinifex Press).

Joan Newmann
(1942-)

Poet and teacher. Born in Tandragee, County Armagh, she was educated in Portadown, Belfast and at Queen's University, Belfast. She taught English in various schools in Ulster and has worked for the Workers' Educational Association. She was a member of the Philip Hobsbaum Belfast Writers' Group in the 1960s, and the Queen's University Festival published a pamphlet of her poetry, *First Letter Home*, in 1965. This was followed by *Suffer Little Children* from Diamond Publications, University of Ulster (1992) and *Circumcision Party* from Honest Ulsterman Publications, Belfast (1995). Her poetry has appeared in many anthologies including *Young Commonwealth Poets* (Heineman, 1965), *Word of Mouth* (Blackstaff, 1996) and *Signals* (Abbey Press, Newry, 1997). She has been widely published since 1965 in magazines and journals such as *Poetry, Atlanta Review, Honest Ulsterman, Poetry Ireland Review, Verse, Fortnight* and *The Cúirt Journal*. She has given readings internationally. In 1999, with her daughter Kate Newmann, she opened a publishing house, Summer Palace Press. She is a member of the Word of Mouth poetry collective. The world of her poetry is that experienced as daughter, mother and intimate friend. Each poem relies on the senses to bring her reader close to her clear-eyed vision and rich female emotional life.

POETRY COLLECTIONS

Coming of Age. (1995). Belfast, The Blackstaff Press.
Thin Ice. (1998). Newry, County Down, Abbey Press.

REMEMBERING BRIDGET CLEARY

for Adrienne Maher

At mystery of moonless night:
A white horse shivering its skin between her knees.

Through shuttered window – locked door
They listened – tortured pleas between gargled screams:
John Dunne, his mountainy herbal medicine,
Forcing metallic spoons between her adamant teeth;
Clapping his big-boned hand across her mouth
Till scare in her eyes of smothering
Brought stillness. Men trapping her feet,
Shrieks of 'bitch' from the man she married,
Imprint of hot poker on her forehead part concealed by soot.

Not even the first time they held her on the grate –
Shallow-breathing of watchers
Waiting for the djinn to leave her –
Her shouting, 'Would you scorch me like a herring?'

No sullen smoulder of late-night turf
When she was laid to burn, belly down,
Her perfect human head fogged in agony.

'She's gone with the evil back to her own.'
As they frantically dug drenched peat,
Her slung body displacing chill brown bog-water.

Breaking, bruising, burning in her:
Free bareback woman
Out-cantering fearsome night.

Colette Nic Aodha
(1967-)

Poet and teacher. Born in County Galway, she was raised in County Mayo and educated in the Presentation College, Headford, County Galway. She received a BA degree in Irish and History from University College, Galway in 1988. After further training, she began her teaching career in 1990. She writes in both Irish and English. She was a prizewinner in the Dún Laoghaire Poetry Festival of 1993. Her work has been published in *Poetry Ireland*, *The Cúirt Journal*, *Comhar*, *Feasta*, *An tUltach*, *Lá*, *Samhlaíocht Aniar*, and *Writing In The West*. The Irish language poet Deirdre Brennan has praised her poetry for its quiet lyricism, "in tune with its surroundings." Nic Aodha read at the 1999 Cúirt International Festival of Literature, Galway.

POETRY COLLECTION

Baill Seirce. (1998). Baile Átha Cliath, Coiscéim.

BARR TAOIDE

Is cuan mé.
Feicim radharcanna áille na mara
Chuile lá

Is mé ag breathnú amach
Thar chraiceann na gcurach
Scaipthe ar an trá.

Tagann tú isteach
Ar gach barra taoide
Ag caitheamh smionagair uait.

Nílim i mbaol
Fad is atá uisce
Ag rith im chuisle.

HIGH TIDE

I am a harbour
I see beautiful oceanscapes
each day

as I peer
over the skin of currachs
strewn on the beach.

You come ashore
at each high tide
scattering your debris.

I am safe
as long as water
pulsates in my veins.

trans. author

Máire Áine Nic Gearailt

(1946-)

 Poet, prose writer and teacher. Born in County Kerry, she was educated in St. Ita's College, Dingle, County Kerry and trained as a Primary Teacher in Mary Immaculate Training College, Limerick. She later trained as a remedial teacher and received an MA degree from the National University of Ireland, Maynooth where she now lectures. Her poems have been published in the Irish language publications *Innti*, *Feasta* and *Comhar*. She has also had essays and poetry published in *Iris Chonradh na Gaeilge* (The Gaelic League magazine, New York), in the anthology *Nua-Fhilí III*, *The Kerryman*, *Anois* and *Inniu*. She has been awarded many Oireachtas prizes for her poetry and her poems have been on the school syllabus for some years.

POETRY COLLECTIONS

Éiric Uachta. (1971). Baile Átha Cliath, Coiscéim.
An tUlchabhán agus Dánta Eile. (1990). Baile Átha Cliath, Coiscéim.
Leaca Liombó (1990). Baile Átha Cliath, Coiscéim.
Mo chúis bheith beo. (1991). Baile Átha Cliath, Coiscéim.
Ó Ceileadh an Bhreasaíl. (1992). Baile Átha Cliath, Coiscéim.

TEICHEADH

Níl le déanamh ach géilleadh
Do shruth na farraige seo
Gabháil go réidh le rabharta na mblian –
Le suaitheadh is tarraingt na haoise
I dtreo caoinché ónar seoladh fadó riamh
I ngleoiteog an dóchais.

Ó ceileadh an Bhreasaíl i mbroinn na mara
Níor bádh de thaisme criú an aonair
I bhfad ó bhaile buaileadh talamh
I mball strainséartha.

I gcathair an láithrigh, cuirtear glas ar dhóirse
Mall san oíche
Is i gcónaí i suan, cloistear cnead na taoide
Faoi bhun na bfaill isteach
Ar thonn tuile na fáistine suíonn fidléir –
ldir chodladh is dhúiseacht
Cloistear a phort ar an ngaoith ....

Ar líonra na haimsire
Beirtear isteach
I mbarróg an tsáile sínte amach
Aghaidh ar ché na macallaí.

FLIGHT

There is nothing to do except to cede
To this current
To calmly go with the flow of the years –
With the turmoil and pull of time
Towards a gentle harbour set out from long ago
In the sailboat of hope.

Since Hy-Brazil hid in the ocean's depths
No accident befell this crew of one
Dry dock was reached far away
In a place of strangers.

In the city of the present, doors are secured
Late at night
And always in sleep the panting tide is heard
Beneath the cliffs sucked in
On the tidal wave of the future a fiddler sits –
Between sleeping and waking
His tune is heard on the wind ---

Embracing the overflowing time
Lying in the crested waves
Facing that harbour of echoes.

trans. author.

Eiléan Ní Chuilleanáin

(1942-)

Poet, lecturer and editor. Born in Cork, one of three children of the late Eilís Dillon (novelist and critic) and Cormac Ó Chuilleanáin, Professor of Irish at University College, Cork. She was educated in University College, Cork where she received degrees in literature and history. She later studied Elizabethan literature at Oxford. A lecturer in English and Fellow of Trinity College, Dublin, she is, with her husband Macdara Woods, one of the four founder-editors of *Cyphers*. In 1973 she won the Patrick Kavanagh Award and was short-listed for *The Irish Times* – Aer Lingus Award in 1990. She was nominated for the European Literature Prize in 1992 and the Irish-American Cultural Institute awarded her the O'Shaughnessy Prize for Poetry in 1992. Edited Maria Edgeworth's *Belinda* for Everyman Paperback (1993) and *Irish Women: Image and Achievement* (Arlen House, 1985) and co-edited *Noble and Joyous Histories: English Romances, 1375-1650* with J. D. Pheifer, (1993). Resonating with ancient rites and presences from a spiritual otherworld, Ní Chuilleanáin is an intellectually challenging poet whose influence has been important to younger poets and has broadened the scope of Irish poetry, particularly for women.

POETRY COLLECTIONS

Acts and Monuments. (1972). Dublin, The Gallery Press.
Site of Ambush. (1975). Dublin, The Gallery Press.
The Second Voyage. (1977). Dublin, The Gallery Press /
    Winston-Salem, N.C., Wake Forest University Press.
    2nd edition, Dublin, The Gallery Press, 1986 / Winston Salem,
    N.C., Wake Forest University Press, 1989.

The Rose-Geranium. (1981). Dublin, The Gallery Press /
    Cork, Cork University Press.
The Magdalene Sermon. (1989). Dublin, The Gallery Press.
The Magdalene Sermon and Other Poems. (1991).
    Winston-Salem, N.C., Wake Forest University Press.
The Brazen Serpent. (1994). Oldcastle, County Meath,
    The Gallery Press.

ASTRAY

When I heard the voice on the radio
All of a sudden announcing the captives were free
I was holding my young cousin
Forcibly down with two arms
Gripping him back from the street
Where he wanted to flatten himself
Under the wheels of the cars.
I waited for the dose to work
And tried to make out what he had been wearing
Half-recognising shreds of denim
An old velvet shirt of my own.

Next week the men were back
Bigger than we remembered
Sitting shakily in the kitchen –
The table a midden of crumbs and documents –
Getting up in the long silences
To carry a cup to the sink
And wash it very carefully.
He stayed upstairs all May.

In June when the raspberries were in
They started to help with the picking
And after that the apples –
They spent days up the ladders
And let us get on with the cooking.

We sat long evenings outside.
But he would not work in the orchard
Or eat with us at meals.

And so it remained, long after
We were used to the loud voices
Hollowing from the fields –
He jumped when he heard them.
You'd find him rarely smoking

In the courtyard by the bins
Reached by the steep back stairs
Where nobody ever came.

And our liberation never
Reached him. He lived on
In a world I could only picture
By thinking of a lost tribe
Astray on a reservation:
No gin and tonic, no
Aspirin, just willow tea.
No tin openers, no mules, no buses,
No Galaico-Portuguese, no Methodists,
No fruit but rotten powdery imploded oranges,
No news from the prison cells.

Nuala Ní Dhomhnaill

(1952-)

 Poet and teacher. Born in Lancashire, England and raised in Chorca Dhuibhne, an Irish speaking district (Gaeltacht) of County Kerry. She graduated with a BA degree from University College, Cork in 1972, and received her Higher Diploma in Education the following year. She spent some years living in Turkey before she settled in Dublin. She writes only in the Irish language, although her work is widely translated by such writers as Michael Hartnett and Paul Muldoon. In her unique style of writing she contrasts the commonplace with images of strong women, goddesses and queens from folklore. Awarded many prizes for her poetry, nationally and internationally, she currently tutors in Boston College, USA, a position which reflects her status as a highly valued international poet. She is one of Ireland's most gifted and celebrated poets writing in Irish in this century.

POETRY COLLECTIONS

An Dealg Droighin. (1981). Baile Átha Cliath agus Corcaigh, Cló Mercier.
Féar Suaithinseach. (1984). Maigh Nuad, An Sagart.
Selected Poems: Trans. Michael Hartnett. (1996). Raven Arts Press, Dublin.
Pharaoh's Daughter. (1990). Oldcastle, County Meath, The Gallery Press.
Feis. (1991). Maigh Nuad, An Sagart.
The Astrakhan Cloak. (1992). Oldcastle, County Meath, The Gallery Press / North Carolina, Wake Forest Press.
Spíonáin is Róiseanna. (1993). Indreabhán, Conamara, Cló Iar Chonnachta.
Selected Poems: Rogha Dánta. (1993). Baile Átha Cliath, New Island Books.
Cead Aighneas. (1998). An Daingean, An Sagart.
The Water Horse. (1999). Oldcastle, County Meath, The Gallery Press.

TUSA

Is tusa, pé thú féin,
an fíréan
a thabharfadh cluais le héisteacht,
b'fhéidir, do bhean inste scéil
a thug na cosa léi, ar éigean,
ó láthair an chatha.

Níor thugamair féin an samhradh linn
ná an geimhreadh.
Níor thriallamair ar bord loinge
go Meiriceá ná ag lorg ár bhfortúin
le chéile i slí ar bith
ins na tíortha teo thar lear.

Níor ghaibheamair de bharr na gcnoc
ar chapall láidir álainn dubh.
Níor luíomair faoi chrann caorthainn
is an oíche ag cur cuisne.
Ní lú ná mar a bhí tinte cnámh
is an adharc á séideadh ar thaobh na gréine.

Eadrainn bhí an fharraige mhór
atá brónach. Eadrainn
bhí na cnoic is na sléibhte
ná casann ar a chéile.

YOU ARE

Whoever you are, you are
The real thing. The witness
Who might lend an ear
To a woman with a story
Barely escaped with her life
From the place of battle.
Spring the sweet spring was not sweet for us
Nor winter neither
We never stepped aboard a ship together
Bound for America to seek
Our fortune, we never
Shared those hot foreign lands.

We did not fly over the high hills
Riding the fine black stallion,
Or lie under the hazel branches
As the night froze about us,
No more than we lit bonfires of celebration
Or blew the horn on the mountainside.

Between us welled the ocean
Waves of grief. Between us
The mountains were forbidding
And the roads long, with no turning.

trans. Eiléan Ní Chuilleanáin.

Máirín Ní Dhomhnalláin
(1914-)

Poet and scholar. Born in County Sligo, she was educated in Scoil Chaitríona, Dublin and at University College, Dublin. She graduated with degrees in Celtic Studies and Early Modern Irish and worked from 1937-1979 in the Library of the Royal Irish Academy in Dublin. She published articles on the Old Irish Manuscripts in the Irish language newspaper *Inniu* during the 1960s and her poetry has been published in *Comhar*, *Feasta*, *The Hawthorn*, *Samlaíocht Aniar* and *Podium*. Her poetic themes are nature and history. She blends them into a poetry full of musical richness.

POETRY COLLECTION

Sin Mar a Bhí. (1997). Baile Átha Cliath, Coiscéim.

FEAR AN CHLOCA LÉITH

"Feicfidh tú go fóill i seanteach Seoirseach áirithe
Samhail an mháistir úd a mhair go luath sa chéad
Ag breathnú roimis amach fá éide mhíleata
As fráma darach is déid.
A dhorn ar cholg órtha
Taobh leis an clogad comhraic –
Seanóir airdeallach ard
Le clóca liath foscailte
Is oinigh ar a bhráid.

Tailtí is teach ba leis iad, gach a bhain le tiarna talún,
Cosantóir dlí is teampaill mar ba dhual dá shórt."
"Tailtí is maoin, cén chaoi ar tugadh dó iad?"
"I leabhra staire léirítear an fáth."
"Meas tú ar chuir sé tionóntaí ar deoraíocht?"
"B'fhéidir nár chuir. Ní thig liom féin a rá.
Ach bhí sé cróga, cinnte. Bhí sé réidh
Le troid don Impireacht i gcrích i gcéin,
Ar pháirc an áir.
Ach beart ar son na hÉireann – ní raibh sí riamh sa mheá.
B'shin í an raic a thógfadh clann na meirleach,
An dream a shéan an dlí.
A shamhail ar son na hÉireann ní dhéanfadh seisean di.

An Impireacht le druidim as a chéile,
Cé nár léir dó é,
Nó ridirí na rothar ar a mbealach chun a Sé Déag,
Ag fógairt nua-ré."

THE MAN IN THE GREY CLOAK

"In a certain old Georgian house you still can see
The portrait of that master who lived early in the century,
Looking straight ahead in military uniform
Out of an oaken and ivory frame.
His hand on a gilded sword – hilt,
The battle – helmet beside him –
A tall, watchful elderly man
In an open grey cloak
[That reveals] the decorations on his breast.

He owned the house and lands, and all the appurtenances of
a landlord,
He was a protector of the law and of the Church as was his
hereditary right."
"Land and property, how were they given to him?"
"You will find the explanation in the history books."
"Do you think that he sent tenants into exile?"
"Perhaps not. I cannot say for sure.
But he was brave, certainly. He was prepared
To fight for the Empire in a distant land,
On the battle-field.
But [such] a deed for Ireland's sake never occurred to him.
That was the riot that the rebels raised,
The mob that spurned the law.
Such a deed he would not do for Ireland.

The Empire on the verge of collapse,
But that he could not foresee
nor the bicycle knights on their road to Nineteen – Sixteen
announcing a new era."

trans. author.

Colette Ní Ghallchóir
(1950-)

Poet and teacher. She was born in the Bluestack Mountains, County Donegal. Her family later moved north to the Bloody Foreland area of Donegal. She trained as a teacher and worked in a Primary School in Letterkenny. Her work was included in the Celtic anthology *Writing the Wind*, published by New Native Press in the USA (1997). In 1998 she was published as one of six emerging poets by Cló Iar-Chonnachta in the anthology *An Chéad Chló*. She was nominated for a Pushkin Award in 1996 for her interest in developing children's writing in schools. Her work has appeared in many of the prominent journals and magazines in this country. Her poetry has all the qualities of having sprung from the richest oral tradition.

POETRY COLLECTION
Idir Dhá Ghleann. (1999). Baile Átha Cliath, Coiscéim.

I NGAIRDIN NA N-ÚLL

Dá mbeinn óg arís,
Is tusa óg arís
I nGairdín na n-Úll

Do bhronnfainn ort
An t-úll ba dheirge
Ar an gcrann

Go bhfeicfinn
An tsolas,
Mar lasair thintrí
i do shúile.

Bheadh fuaim
Na Toirní
Amuigh adaí
idir na hAchlaí

'S muidne,
Ar ár suaimhneas
Ag dáileadh na dtorthaí
b'aibí ar a chéile
Ceann ar cheann.

IN THE GARDEN OF APPLES

If I were young again
and you were young again
in the garden of apples,
I would give to you the reddest
apple on the bough.
Thunder would roar its way, out yonder,
between Achla Mór and Achla Beag:
but you and I would be happy
sharing the ripest apples with each other –
one by one.

trans. Barbara Parkinson.

Áine Ní Ghlinn

(1955-)

Poet and journalist. Born in County Tipperary, the youngest of five children, she was educated in Presentation College, Thurles and at University College, Dublin where she received a BA degree and a Diploma in Higher Education. Working as a broadcaster with RTÉ and Raidio na Gaeltachta, she lectures part-time in Dublin City University. Her poetry has been anthologised, included in text books and broadcast on radio and television. She won Oireachtas awards in 1985 and 1987 and Duais Bhord na Gaeilge at Listowel Writers' Week in 1987. Her poems focus mainly on themes of emigration and child sexual abuse. Tough and uncompromisingly direct while maintaining a lyricism, this poet deals openly, and like no other contemporary Irish poet, with subjects which are often taboo.

POETRY COLLECTIONS

An Chéim Bhriste. (1984). Baile Átha Cliath, Coiscéim.
Gairdín Pharthais agus dánta eile. (1988). Baile Átha Cliath, Coiscéim.
Deora Nár Caoineadh – Unshed Tears. (1996). Baile Átha Cliath, Coiscéim / The Dedalus Press.

TU FÉIN IS MÉ FÉIN

Thógamar teach féir – tú féin is mé féin – ag
bun an mhóinéir. Do thrí scór bliain dod chromadh
ach fós bhí na ballaí chomh hard liom féin.

Chnag tú ar chloch an dorais. Bhuail isteach.
"Mise Daidí, tusa Mam," a dúirt go séimh, "is mé
ag filleadh ort tar éis obair an lae." D'ólamar
tae as cupáin bheaga bhréige.
"Téanam ort, a chroí. Tá sé in am luí. Bain
díot." Is bhain. Bhain tú piliúr as balla na
cistine. Do thrí scór bliain dom phlúchadh.

D'éiríomar. Ghlan le do chiarsúr mé. Phóg mo
chuid fola leis an gcréacht a leigheas is
d'fhilleamar – tú féin is mé féin – ar theach
mo mháthar, ar theach d'iníne.

Ach pé sracfhéachaint a thugaim thar mo ghuaille
feicim fós ó am go chéile an chréacht oscailte
a d'fhág tú i mballa na cistine.

YOURSELF AND MYSELF

We built a grass house – yourself and myself –
at the foot of the meadow. You hunched under your
three score years. Me no higher than the walls.

You knocked on our stone door. You came in.
"I'll be Daddy, you be Mam," you said softly,
"and I'll be coming home from my day's work."
We drank tea out of little toy cups.

"Come on, love. It's time for bed. Strip off, now."
I stripped. You plucked a pillow from the kitchen
wall. Your three score years stifling me.

We got up. You cleaned me with your handkerchief.
You kissed my blood to heal the wound and we
went home – yourself and myself – to my mother's,
your daughter's, house.

But whatever glance I throw over my shoulder
I still can see, from time to time, the gaping
wound you left in the kitchen wall.

trans. author.

Brighid Ní Mhóráin

(1951-)

 Poet, prose writer and teacher. Born in County Cork, she was educated in Tralee and at University College, Cork. She was awarded a BA degree and a Higher Diploma in Education in 1975. In 1985 she received a diploma for Linguistics and in 1990 a M. Litt. in Irish from Trinity College, Dublin. She is currently a language teacher in Tralee. Her poetry has been included in anthologies and has been broadcast on Raidio na Gaeltachta and Radio Kerry and has appeared in *Innti, Ultach* and in *Women's Work*. She was a prizewinner in Oireachtas competitions, in 1988 and 1989.

POETRY COLLECTION

Ceiliúradh Cré. (1992). Baile Átha Cliath, Coiscéim.

AN COSÁN BÁN

Pós fear ón sliabh
is pósfair faill is garbhach
ná cothódh an naosc
nó an giorria rua
le linn dúluachair.
Íosfair picil an challshaotha
an dá lá déag is an fhaid a mhairfir;
nuair a shínfidh searc do chléibhe
led' thaobh ar thocht an anró
ní fada go mbeidh clipeadh is crá
in áit mhil na bpóg, a dúradar.

Ba dhána an té
'thabharfadh a ndúshlán,
a ghrá dhil dhuibh,
      'gus a shiúlódh le d'ais
ar an gCosán Bán
go Cnoc na Naomh
– ach ní domsa do b'aithreach.

Ba féileacán é m'anam
ag blaistínteacht ó luibh go bláth;
ba leasc liom buanchumann a cheangal
gur thairgís dom deoch
ó thobar gan bhonn do ghrá,
– ach chonac scáil id' shúile a mheall mé,
bhuaileas mo bhéal ar an uisce
is thánag go sochma
i dtearmann do sheirce.

THE WHITE PATH

Marry the man from the mountain
and you'll wed cliff and moorland
that wouldn't feed the snipe
or the red hare
when rushes blacken.
You'll eat the pickle of hardship
every day that you live;
with your heart's love lying
beside you on the bed of want
it won't be long 'til rows
replace honeyed kisses, they said.

It's a bold one
would challenge them
my dear, dark love
and walk by your side
on the White Path
to the hill of the saints,
– but I don't regret it.

My butterfly soul flitted
sipping from herb and flower,
loathe to be tied down
until you offered me a drink
from the well that never runs dry,
but the shadow in your eyes drew me.
I put my lips to the water
and came so gently
into love's sanctuary.

trans. author.

Jean O'Brien

(1952-)

Poet. Born in Dublin. She was a founding member of the Dublin Writers' Workshop, and has published her poems in their workshop journals. Her poetry has also appeared in *Poetry Ireland Review, Gown, Fortnight, Irish Studies Review* (UK) and the *Cloverdale Anthology*. In 1990 she was awarded a scholarship to the Eastern Washington University workshop in Dublin. She has read widely in Ireland and has been broadcast on RTÉ Radio 1. In 1992 her pamphlet *Working the Flow* was published by Lapwing Publications, Belfast. Her poetry explores themes of family and personal relationships. Her working out of the mother/daughter relationship gave her many poems which are uncompromising, honest and unsentimental.

POETRY COLLECTION

The Shadow Keeper. (1997). Galway, Salmon Publishing.

THE GATES OF HORN
for Sylvia Plath

I type in Arial to give the words
a breathing space –
open like red tulips
to her hurt lines. Lady Lazarus
in the hospital bed,

doing what she did best, again
and again. Her skin stretched
on a wire frame, O the light,
it was lovely, but it hurt her, the red
was too much.

The tulips almost touched her
with one eye firmly on the sky
looking for the unmiraculous, winged
woman, her stamen rising
to the stings.

* *this spelling of Arial is a typeface*

Julie O'Callaghan

(1954-)

Poet. Born in Chicago, she now lives in Ireland and works in the Library of Trinity College, Dublin. Her first collection, *Edible Anecdotes*, was a Poetry Book Society Recommendation and her second, *What's What*, was a Poetry Book Society Choice. She was awarded Irish Arts Council bursaries in 1985, 1990 and 1998. Her poetry is represented in many British and Irish publications, including *The Observer, The Times Literary Supplement, The Irish Times, Poetry Ireland Review* and *The New Statesman*. She is published in the USA in such magazines as *The Atlanta Review*. She reads at festivals and in schools and has been broadcast on radio and television. Her observations of life are delivered with sharp wit and a wicked gift for mimicry. She writes for young people, is widely anthologised and is represented in *The New Oxford Book of Children's Verse*. Her poetry appears in school texts in Ireland, Britain and Canada. Whether set in her native Chicago or in her adopted Dublin, her poems explore contemporary life with an imagination that is both entertaining and accurate.

POETRY COLLECTIONS

Edible Anecdotes. (1983). Dublin, The Dolmen Press.
Bright Lights Blaze Out. (1986). Oxford, Oxford University Press.
Taking My Pen for a Walk. (1988). London, Orchard Books.
What's What. (1991). Newcastle Upon Tyne, Bloodaxe Books.
Two Barks. (1998). Newcastle upon Tyne, Bloodaxe Books.

THE GREAT BLASKET ISLAND

Six men born on this island
have come back after twenty-one years.
They climb up the overgrown roads
to their family houses
and come out shaking their heads.
The roofs have fallen in
and birds have nested in the rafters.
All the white-washed rooms
all the nagging and praying
and scolding and giggling
and crying and gossiping
are scattered in the memories of these men.
One says, 'Ten of us, blown to the winds –
some in England, some in America, some in Dublin.
Our whole way of life – extinct.'
He blinks back the tears
and looks across the island
past the ruined houses, the cliffs
and out to the horizon.

Listen, mister, most of us cry sooner or later
over a Great Blasket Island of our own.

Clairr O'Connor

(1951-)

 Poet, novelist, playwright, teacher. Born in Limerick and educated at University College, Cork where she received a degree in Medieval History and English. Later she received post-graduate diplomas in Education and Japanese Studies at St. Patrick's College, Maynooth. She lives and teaches in Dublin. She has written plays, poetry, short stories and novels. Her poetry has been anthologised and broadcast, and she gives readings extensively in Ireland and in the USA. In 1988 she was the Irish Exchange Writer at New Dramatists in New York. Her novel *Belonging* (1991) was nominated for *The Irish Times*/Aer Lingus Award. She is one of the writers included in *The Great Book of Ireland*, the unique vellum manuscript of the work of poets and artists assembled to represent the best in contemporary Irish cultural life. She was chairwoman of the Irish Writers' Centre, 1994-1996. She brings both anger and tenderness to the theme of love in her poems which is expressed in a short, free-verse style. When she writes of motherhood and home she draws her readers directly into the experiences without sentimentality.

POETRY COLLECTION

When You Need Them. (1989). Galway, Salmon Publishing.

OUTCAST ELDER

I have put aside
the crested head-dress
I no longer raise
the cross-hatching
spear. They buried
my troubled drums
under the eucalyptus.
A fire-spitter no more,
I do not jump the fire
flames or lie by my wife.

When the snow melts
she will be new-bedded
and my masks will make
her wedding fire.
Her new mask will be
of antelope and her tent
fires will be lit by
elders' wives.
She will sing for the chameleon.

Her colours will mirror
sky and river. But I will
remember how her hands
held the clay pot.

Mary O'Donnell

(1954-)

Poet, fiction writer and critic. Born in County Monaghan, she was educated at the St. Louis Convent and at St. Patrick's College, Maynooth from where she graduated in Philosophy and German. She was writer-in-residence in UCD in 1994 and was drama critic for *The Sunday Tribune* from 1988-1990. She scripted and presented the RTÉ Radio 1 poetry request programme 'Along the Backwater' from 1992-1994. Her poetry has been published widely in Irish, British and US magazines, journals and anthologies. She was twice nominated for an *Irish Times/Aer Lingus Award* (1991 and 1998) and was a prizewinner at Listowel Writers' Week, in the Patrick Kavanagh Poetry Competition (1986), the Bloodaxe National Poetry Competition and won many other awards. The recipient of an Arts Council Bursary in 1992, she is also an award-winning short-fiction writer and a best-selling novelist. She has translated Portuguese, French and Dutch poetry and is preparing a translation of Ingeborg Bachmann's selected poems. Her critical work, fiction, lecturing and journalism together with her poetry have been an important part of the cultural life of Ireland for many years and she is considered one of the country's most exciting talents.

POETRY COLLECTIONS

Reading the Sunflowers in September. (1990). Galway, Salmon Publishing.
Spiderwoman's Third Avenue Rhapsody. (1993). Galway, Salmon Publishing.
Unlegendary Heroes. (1998). County Clare, Salmon Publishing.

IN THE TUILERIES

We misjudged the scale of things.
Two fifteen or thereabouts, we'd said.
Once off the *rue de Rivoli*, I knew
that we would wander without meeting.
I sat a while, back to the sun,
watched children send wooden sailboats
jagging at the ornamental pond,
hoped that you'd be drawn to those
who idled near the brittle floats.
An icy autumn day, lethal winds
in a high, blue sky drove fruits
and leaves to withdraw and sink deep.
No reference to a world rank
with injustice, no sense of all the wrongs
and all that stank about the universe.
Here, a place we'd read about,
a novelistic arena, a moment in a season,
where, eternally, dogs and women breeze
by as if on wheels, and silent couples stroll
the yellowed grit between the trees,
and white-shod tourists like ourselves,
revisit all the chapters that they must.
We balanced as never before, but separately.
In all that vastness between us,
no exclaiming on symmetry or stone,
on sculpture or period; comfort for sure,
in a city endowed, but alone
with orangeries, trim trees in view;
the grand line of paths extended perspectives
beyond the usual limits. You felt it too,
I discovered later, and absence, as if
we'd inadvertently cleared the wrong fence,
then herded one another, prematurely, set to fail,
towards some final mortal innocence.
As so often, we misjudged the scale.

Kathleen O'Driscoll

(1941-)

 Poet and fiction writer. Born in Cork she was educated at Taylor' Hill Convent, Galway and Our Lady's School, Dublin and Wicklow. She later received a degree in Modern Languages at University College, Galway and worked as a teacher. Her short story collection *Ether* was published in 1981 and her poetry and stories were published and broadcast, locally and nationally. Two of her poems appear in A.A. Kelly's *Pillars of the House,* 1987. She has read in schools under two Arts Council writers-in-schools schemes. Themes in her poetry are political, satirical and personal. In more recent years she has worked on script, direction, camera and editing at Galway Resource Centre. *Berlin Blues,* a film she wrote, shot and directed, in Galway and Berlin, won first prize at the Cork Film Festival. She continues to work in film and to write poetry.

POETRY COLLECTION

Goodbye Joe. (1981). Dublin, Caledon.

WAR CHILD

Little matchstick man
It never was my plan to leave you screaming at the thunder.
Rain and words and lightning
Mixed to nightmare pitch,
Your skinny awkward legs
Flailing the clouds.
Gun bursts burning haunted eyes
That should be younger, tranquil.
Will you forgive me, little matchstick man?

My plans were oh so grand
If you could understand
I dreamed a perfect world for kids like you,
Where greed and prejudice
Would be impossible
And only joy could burn.
And I'm not strong as heroes from kids stories
Who could rescue you.
From human tragedy.
Will you believe I never meant to crack with fear?

Small broken bird
I'm just a bigger helpless creature
With broken hopes.
Will you forgive me, little broken child?

Sheila O'Hagan

(1933-)

Poet. Born in Dublin. Emigrated to London at the age of nineteen and studied at Birkbeck College, London University where she received degrees in Art, English Literature and Theatre. She began to write poetry in 1986 and won the Goldsmith Award 1988. She won the first of her four Listowel Writers' Week prizes in 1988. In 1991 she won the Patrick Kavanagh Award and in 1992 *The Sunday Tribune* Hennessy Award for New Irish Poet of the Year. Widely published and anthologised in Ireland, Britain, Canada, Australia and the USA in publications such as *Poetry Ireland Review*, *Poetry Wales*, *Envoi* and *The Maryland Poetry Review*, she has also broadcast and appeared on television. She returned to live in Dublin in 1990 and was writer-in-residence for County Kildare in 1995. Medbh McGuckian has said of her poetry that "in line with Seamus Heaney's *Seeing Things*, her poetry puts the faculty of vision back at the heart of 'the brighter fire' of the poetic venture." Her interests in Irish history and literature, the visual arts and theatre are all hallmarks of this poet's work.

POETRY COLLECTIONS

The Peacock's Eye. (1992). Galway, Salmon Publishing.
The Troubled House. (1995). Galway, Salmon Publishing.

THE RETURN OF ODYSSEUS TO ITHACA

When he limped home smelling of the world, stood under
The great gate of the courtyard, shreds of vigour
In the wiry hair, the ageing limbs still sinewed,
She saw him from her window, knew she'd acted right
But hard with anger for the loveless wait, withdrew
Into the shadows of her room, for three days cried
To her unborn sons, counted the twenty notches
On the olive post he'd hewn and whittled for their bed,
Heard his bellowed rage from the old banquet hall
Swagger of the warrior his dander up, thud of crossbolt
Cudgelled skulls, blood on the tapestries, and when
His anger spent, he leant exhausted by the fireplace
She fixed her face and hair, came down to him, cradled
His fading manhood and drew the sting of their lost years.

Nessa O'Mahoney

(1964-)

Poet. Born in Dublin and was educated in St. Louis High School, Rathmines and in University College, Dublin. She has worked in journalism and public relations. Her poetry has appeared in Irish, British, Italian and US publications including *Poetry Ireland Review, Fortnight, Windows, The Sunday Tribune, Agenda, Iota* and *The Atlanta Review*. She has broadcast on RTÉ Radio 1 and presents a radio programme on creative writing for Anna Livia FM. Joint winner of the Kerry International Summer School (K.I.S.S.) Poetry Competition in 1996, she was also a prizewinner in The Patrick Kavanagh Awards. In 1997 she won the National Women's Poetry Competition and was short-listed for *The Sunday Tribune/* Hennessy New Irish Writing Award. She currently works for the Irish Arts Council. Themes in her poetry include memory, love and family relationships.

POETRY COLLECTION
Bar Talk. (1999). Dublin, iTaLiCs Press.

LAMENT FOR A SHY MAN

He would have hated this,
the man who turned his face
to hedgerows rather than risk
a greeting on a country road.
It would be another death
to know the details of his life
were being discussed over
breakfast, at church gates,
in hazy snugs as far as
Moate and Mullingar.

Mary O'Malley

(1954-)

 Poet and teacher. Born in Connemara where she grew up. She was educated at University College, Galway where she received a degree in English. She taught in London and at the New University of Lisbon. She has served as a member of the organising committee of the Cúirt International Festival of Literature, Galway. She has been writer-in-residence in Derry and Mayo and has edited two collections of writing by young people. She received a Hennessy Award in 1990 and Arts Council bursaries in 1992 and 1995. She has broadcast and appeared on television, and travels in Europe and the USA, giving readings and lectures. In 1998 she was elected a member of Aosdána. Widely published and anthologised, her poetry is imbued with a sense of the West of Ireland, its traditions and cultures. The late George MacBeth has said of her work: "These are the poems of a traveller seeking happiness, and charting the obstacles to her search as she finds them." A highly individual poetic identity drives her poetry.

POETRY COLLECTIONS

A Consideration of Silk. (1990). Galway, Salmon Publishing.
Where the Rocks Float. (1993). Galway, Salmon Publishing.
The Knife in the Wave. (1997). County Clare, Salmon Publishing.

FATE

After Caitlín Maude

If this rusted petal could moisten and tint
I'd have a hundred blinded girls

Weave a silk carpet for your feet. You'd walk
In and gossip for hours, sitting cross-legged.

If it could find its way back
Even to the original rose

Your footsteps would still blaze
Out across the world.

You would leave your lover's bed refreshed
And come home to sleep in his arms.

But no. The hawthorn has stopped
In mid flowering, as if recalled

And you, Caitlín, will stay
The dark side of the glass, a watcher.

This petal will not find a place
Among her rustling sisters.

It too will remain what it is:
A memento mori, like all love tokens.

Barbara Parkinson

(1952-)

Poet and playwright. Born in Galway, she was educated at Galway Regional Technical College where she studied Science. She lives in Killybegs, County Donegal and is a member of the Killybegs Writers' Group. Nominated for a Hennessy Award in 1992, she was also awarded a prize in the 1993 Patrick Kavanagh Awards. Short-listed for the Open American Poetry Competition in 1994, she was nominated as Poet of the Year 1995 by the International Society of Poets, USA. Her radio play *Choice* was nominated for the P. J. O'Connor Awards in 1992. She has published her poetry in magazines and anthologies in Ireland and in the USA, and has also won several other Irish literary awards, including Donegal Poet of the Year in 1983. A popular reader at festivals and summer schools, she was awarded an Arts Council Bursary in Literature in 1996. John F. Deane has said of her poetry: "The imaginative leaps are intimidating, like the ocean, but yield their treasure to those who seek them." She writes love poetry with a strong physical awareness that is both tender and moving.

POETRY COLLECTION

Any Change for the Jugglers and Other Poems. (1995). Galway, Salmon Publishing.

LEAVING IS THE PRICE

With the energy of a thief
I kneel away the night
in the language of prayer.

But how do I chew on bones
in a saw-dust restaurant
and know they are spare ribs –

slide 'Absolut' down my throat –
compare you to the moon
resting on my shoulder and know

Jesus has not forgotten me –
how do I register a smile and hold it
in some New Year's town –

Stop my soul's maladies that speak
across my so distant flesh –
resist the fruits of rough altars and promise

not to die a good looking corpse?
Soon, then, I hear your words on the wind
right after you have screamed;

I call on the moon to stitch them
as they settle softly in my eyes.
What a demanding river they will make!

Evangeline Paterson
(1928-)

 Poet. Born in Limavady, County Derry. She grew up in Dublin and is now living in Newcastle upon Tyne. Edited *Other Poetry* magazine in Leicester from 1979 to 1989, and recently revived it in Newcastle. She won the Cheltenham Prize for Poetry in 1980 and her collection *Lucifer At the Fair* was shortlisted for the Forward prize in 1992. Anthologised in many magazines in Britain and the USA, she also wrote one prose work, *What to do with your Poems* (1991). Before the Dedalus Press, Dublin published her first collection to appear in Ireland, she had already published several collections of poetry with the British Taxus Press. Her clear accessible poems written in a lyric voice are never sentimental, never lapse into clíche. That her work has not appeared in Irish literary magazines or anthologies is a loss to Irish readers. The British poet Anne Stevenson, writing of her work, said: "In a just world, her books would sell in thousands; her popularity among those who still believe poetry can be a comprehensible and entertaining art is assured."

POETRY COLLECTIONS

Bringing the Water Hyacinth to Africa. (1983). Newcastle upon Tyne, Taxus Press.
Lucifer at the Fair. (1991). Newcastle upon Tyne, Taxus Press.
Lucifer, with Angels. (1994). Dublin, The Dedalus Press.
A Game of Soldiers. (1997). Exeter, Devon, Stride Publications.

VISITATION

'Have you heard of angels?' said the visiting lady
to the little poor child. 'They have you in their keeping.
They hover around you when your prayers are said.
They whisper dreams in your ear when you are sleeping.'

Said the little poor child, 'I have seen them, tall as gantries
and thick as rain in the air above the town.
They all leaned one way like a field of wheat.
Their faces were white as paper. Their tears fell down.'

Angela Patten

(1952-)

Poet and teacher. Born in Dublin, she grew up in Dun Laoghaire, County Dublin and emigrated to the USA in 1977. She graduated Phi Beta Kappa with a BA in English from The University of Vermont in 1986 and received a Master of Fine Arts in Poetry from Vermont College in 1996. Her poems have appeared in literary magazines in Ireland, Scotland and the USA, and she was a prizewinner in the 1996 Patrick Kavanagh Poetry Competition. A selection of her poems is included in the anthology *Onion River: Six Vermont Poets* (1997). She teaches poetry and gives readings in Vermont and New England and is Development Director of Vermont Arts Council.

POETRY COLLECTION

Still Listening. (1999). County Clare, Salmon Publishing.

AT THE BUTCHER'S SHOP

At age eight I decide I'm a vegetarian
and practice holding my breath
in the butchers' shops so as not to sicken
at the smell of fresh blood and sawdust.
But my mother has a way of collaring me
unexpectedly. Go back to Michael Coyne
the butcher, she says, and tell him
Mrs. Goggins said that meat's too fat.

I traipse up the road to the little row of shops
that face the church. The butcher in a blood-
stained apron is addressing the housewives
like a lover holding his heart out on a plate.
That's a lovely bit of flank steak, Missus,
he cajoles. The women sniff disparagingly,
not wanting to give him an inch for fear
he'll take a mile. I worm my way into the crowd
and repeat my mother's words in a whisper.
The women's heads, sheathed in chiffon
scarves, swivel towards me.

Oh, I'd love to be an angel, a pure spirit
running God's holy messages
instead of standing here without a word
to say for myself, avoiding the glassy stares
of the fish flattened in the window
and the carcases dangling from hooks in the back room.

That's Annie Goggins's young one,
someone says, giving me the once-over.
Annie Swords that was, before she was married.
Imagine being her daughter, I think with horror,
always running to the shops for a stone of coal,
five cigarettes wrapped in tissue paper,
and you can keep the penny for yourself, love.

I shudder as Michael mauls my package
with his bloody hands. Imagine being his daughter,
those fleshy fingers undressing you for bed.
I skedaddle to the door with my pound of flesh
hoping she won't skin me alive
for always accepting whatever I'm handed,
and for having absolutely no backbone.

Anne Peters

(1905-1997)

Poet. Born in Youghal, County Cork. Married in 1939, she accompanied her English husband to the USA, where she experienced life in the oil fields of Oklahoma and Texas. During the war she worked in a factory in England making Spitfires and was a Director of an Allied Forces Centre. She returned to the USA in 1946. She lived in New York City and studied at New York University before moving to Connecticut. Among the anthologies and magazines in which her poetry appeared were: *Poets of Today, The Gardener's Book of Verse, Poetry Ireland Review, The Irish Press, Reality, Manifold, Spirit America*. Her poetry, written in the fifteen years before the publication of her collection *Rings of Green*, was praised by one of England's leading women poets, Kathleen Raine. In North America, the late Louise Townsend Nichol, Vice-President of the Poetry Society of America, described her poetry as "lovely work, beautiful and encompassing." Although Peters spent much of her life away from Ireland, the themes in much of her poetry unmistakably derive from an Irish heritage. Until her death in 1997 she divided her time between Oxford, England and Pocán, County Tipperary.

POETRY COLLECTION

Rings of Green. (1982). Gerrards Cross, Buckinghamshire,
    Colin Smythe Ltd.

THE GREEN MARTYRDOM

Brendan the Voyager, Bishop of Erin,
braving the angry currents
that hissed and coiled like snowy serpents
about rock-skirted Inishmore,
Inishturk, and Inishglora,
brought knowledge of Christ to pagan islanders.
After months of prayer in his homeland
he pushed his coracle ever further
battling the roar-rush of tides
to the rude lands of Alba, Britain and Gaul.
Great hardships of rowing, foundations
of monasteries and schools of learning.

Weary years later, after landing at Fenit,
he retired to his wind-swept hut
atop the cliff-sided peak of Mt. Brenainn.
Many signs, many omens opened visions
as he fasted on berries and water.
One evening, peace overflowing
from the solicitude of stars untarnished
up in the sky heights,
he let thoughts follow each other like feet
striding through his mind, and imbued
by a spirit of penitence, he resolved to break
from all he loved and toil anew among strangers.

And it was morning. He pondered.
Barinthus had told of a vast land
of fruitful trees, herbs, and blossoms,
a paradise hidden behind the ice-mists,
lurking seabeasts, and water-spouting monsters
of the inhospitable Atlantic.
And did not the colonies of terns
that summered around the seaborders
fly away into the sunset each autumn?

Did not the brent-geese that wintered
in the flats and reed-beds of rivers,
fly off into the western horizon each spring?

As a white gull opens its wings
with a loud cry before flight,
Brendan cried aloud:
'God of my brothers, strengthen me!'
Thus, in repentance, and for the sake of others,
he chose the green martyrdom of exile,
to seek the Land of the Many Hues.
In a boat of oxhide, bitumen, and rosin,
back turned to Erin,
he started out across the unknown seas,
aiming toward the bright bed of the sun.

Rosemarie Rowley

(1942-)

Poet. Born in Dublin and educated at Trinity College where she received a degree in English, Philosophy and Irish, followed by a Masters in Literature. Taught in Birmingham and worked with the BBC. Later she worked with the European Parliament in Luxembourg. She has published poetry in underground, alternative and mainstream journals and periodicals in Ireland and abroad since 1960. An essayist, she has contributed reviews and critiques to academic journals and Irish newspapers. She edited *Extended Wings* nos. 1 and 2, community publications from The Rathmines Writers in 1993-94. She was a prizewinner in the 1988 Image Short Story Competition and won first prize in the Scottish International Open Poetry Competition. She read her own poetry and translations from the Irish of women poets of Connaught at the literary celebrations in Thessaloniki, Greece in 1997. Her contribution to contemporary Irish poetry written by women is marked by both her attention to form and her long poems.

POETRY COLLECTIONS

The Broken Pledge and Other Poems. (1985). Dublin, Martello
    Books.
The Sea of Affliction. (1987). Dublin, Rowan Tree Press.
Flight into Reality. (1989). Dublin, Rowan Tree Press.

FAIR-HAIRED DONNCHA
From the Irish

In this small townland happened a wonder
Fair-haired Donncha hanging loose
The death cap on him his hat to sunder
His cravat replaced by a hempen noose

I am approaching in the dead of night
Like a helpless lamb under a flock of sheep
My breast uncovered and my head a fright
To see my dear brother in eternal sleep

I keened the first bout at the head of the lake
And the second long scream at the foot of the gallows
The third agony at the start of the wake
In the midst of strangers, my mouth like aloes

If I had you, where you used belong
Down in Sligo or in the town of the Robe
I would break the gallows, cut the rope strong
And set fair-haired Donncha free from foreign probe

Fair-haired Donncha, it's not the gallows you deserve
Your place at the market and the threshing of corn
North and South, your plough would swerve
Turning the deep red sod upwards to be re-born

Fair-haired Donncha, sweet faithful little brother
I know the people who turned your life to blight
Passing the goblet, reddening the pipe for the other
Waist high in the dew at the ending of the night

You, seed of Mulhaun, misfortunate harbinger of ill
He wasn't an amenable sucker though you got him early
He was a fine figure of a young man, not yours to kill
Who was made for sport and getting sweet sounds from a hurley

O, Fair-haired Donncha, is not death your spancel
In spurs and boots, no ornament you would worsen
I would put fashionable clothes on you, in your everlasting chancel
How I would deck you out as a noble person!

Seed of Mulhaun may your sons be scattered
May your daughters never a dowry seek
The two ends of your table empty and your floor splattered
For my brother you slew, and his fine physique.

The dowry of fair-haired Donncha is coming home, you vandal
And there is no sign of a sheep, a cow, or a horse
But tobacco, pipes and a guttering candle
I won't upbraid them, to grudge would be worse.

Deirdre Shanahan

(1960-)

Poet and fiction writer. Born in London of Irish parents, she studied English at University College, North Wales. Worked as a waitress, stage assistant and teacher. She received an Eric Gregory Award in 1983 and has had poems broadcast on Radio 3's "Poetry Now". Her work has appeared in magazines and journals, including *Poetry Review*, *Encounter*, *Writing Women* and *The Literary Review*. Her eloquent poetic voice is one of dispossession – a mother awakening to the loss of her child, an emigrant exploring her loss of identity away from Ireland. The British poet and critic Christopher Reid has said of her work: "She has a most unusual imagination and her poems are full of intriguing mysteries and sudden, intimate surprises." Her short fiction is now appearing in Britain and in the United States and she gives readings and workshops.

POETRY COLLECTION

Legal Tender. (1988). Hampshire, Enitharmon Press.

LAND

Visiting my father's village
we walked along his field
rented out to a neighbour
whose cattle kept the grass down.
We heard how great-grandfather
returned from gold-prospecting
and bought the land.

Each step on the ridges
was a kind of pilgrimage,
a way of paying respects,
until things changed.
Cows splayed,
the defining path was overgrown
and my father was forced to sell.

At a distance of miles
in his untidy garden of plants
my father turns the soil
with a hurt unhurried eye.
I see strangers work the land,
want to run there so hard
and not come back.

                    *

Intricate thoughts come
to a bending brow
as I write six years on
since moving from Wales
where birds twitched the telegraph lines
and he consumed words.

Leaning against the pink wall
on the mantleshelf, a postcard
of an old man looks out
from the edges, to this world,
angling fingers, steady as chapel walls,
around a cigarette.

reminding me of a cottager
caught in ropes,
lapsing for risks in valleys,
climbing in mist waves
and oceans of endless air,
a voice in resonance and fall,

a handler of words
whose pen wields weight,
ink black as December
carrying thoughts
like a curragh
on a heady sea to the shore.

Janet Shepperson

(1954-)

Poet, fiction writer and teacher. Born in Edinburgh, she received a degree in English from Aberdeen University. She has lived in Belfast since 1977 and has taught creative writing to adult students, and also in the Maze Prison. Her poetry and short stories have been published widely in journals and anthologies, notably the Blackstaff Book of Short Stories (volumes 1 and 2) and Trio 5, also from Blackstaff Press. She was shortlisted twice for a *Sunday Tribune*/Hennessy Award. Two collections of her poetry have been published by Lapwing, Belfast in their pamphlet series, *A Ring with a Black Stone* and *Madonna of the Spaces*. Her poems speak of fear, loss and survival set against the anxiety and sorrow of Northern Ireland. Poems dealing with miscarriage and childlessness are set in landscapes that include urban Belfast and Donegal. She was a prizewinner in the Bridport Arts Centre Creative Writing Competition and has been published in the USA in *The Southern Review* and *The Seneca Review*.

POETRY COLLECTION

The Aphrodite Stone. (1995). Galway, Salmon Publishing.

THE FURTHEST NORTH YOU CAN GO

The wind from the Atlantic's sharp with sleet
that hurls itself against our stinging faces,
and isn't this what we've come to Donegal for –
escape from a place where grief has no rituals
into an icy openness. Here the weather
does our keening for us, and the far
crest of Slieve Snacht against a curdled sky
is pulled towards us by the gleam of snow
as if the wind had snatched handfuls of feathers
to thatch its nest on the bare mountainside.
Along the shore, a scattering of bones.

We stumble over vertebrae, jaws, thighs,
– huge, as if dinosaurs from the last Ice Age
had lumbered here to die. A rutted track
brings loops of rusting wire, shreds of black plastic,
bundles of something bloody roped together,
wedged in the rocks. Carcases. Cattle heads.
Where are the gulls, the stink? Too cold perhaps,
or every edible scrap's been picked – what's left
hasn't the juice to rot, or feed the crows.

Five Finger Strand. Black rocks rear from the sea
in curse or blessing, like a tarnished silver
hand upraised, a reliquary, ancient
and hollow, stuffed with knobs of holy bone.
Malin Head. The cliff path. Flutterings
of white tossed upwards could be seagulls' wings
or foam churned in the whirlpool of Hell's Hole.
We drive back through the mountains. Gusts of snow
surround the car, an endless stream of feathers,
slivers of bone, shimmering, scratching the glass.

Dusk in Belfast. The wind's dropped. Nearly home,
I watch the starlings swirl above the bridges
in hundreds, hordes, a shivering ecstasy
of restlessness, a rustling, drifting mesh
of grey. I think of ashes floating, scattered
with ceremony into the waiting sea.

Jo Slade

(1952-)

Poet and painter. Born in Hertfordshire. Educated at Laurel Hill Convent, Limerick, she studied at the Limerick College of Art, The National College of Art in Dublin and Trinity College. She exhibits her paintings widely and publishes her poetry in journals and anthologies in Ireland and abroad. An editor of an anthology of Limerick writing, *On the Counterscarp: Limerick Writing 1961-1991* (Salmon Publishing). She is also a member of Limerick Fourfront Poets group and works on collaborative poetry. Her poetry has been translated into French, a selection of which is arranged with her paintings in her 1997 publication *Certain Octobers*. Haunting images, wrought into lines of poetry which display her talents in the use of intricate sound patterns, distinguish her as a poet of intensity and powerful imagination.

POETRY COLLECTIONS

In Fields I Hear Them Sing. (1989). Galway, Salmon Publishing.
The Vigilant One. (1994). Galway, Salmon Publishing.
Certain Octobers – Parfois en Octobre. (1997). Galway, Salmon
Publishing / Editions Eireanna, Quimber, France.

FROM WHERE IT CAME

From where it came,
the cold translucent water,
the pain
that nameless flew off

the same moment
a tree
devoured by the sun
in a single gulp
cried out.

From where it came,
that was change
a shattering.
The wood turned to water
became rings
to count days,
the river
the tireless water
that calms me.

From where it came,
out of one
from the smallest
and wood once frail
assumed a permanence.
That was stillness
a completed rhyme
a flower alone
in the blue night.

From where it came,
I saw nothing I was blind
The field emptied
turned to dust.
We obtain grace
we descend gracefully,
we are deeper
than the mercy
shown to us.

Eithne Strong

(1923-1999)

Poet and fiction writer. Born in West County Limerick she received her early education in a breac-Ghaeltacht (an area where Irish language expressions freely blended with spoken English). In 1942, she joined the Irish language movement in Dublin and published her first poetry in Irish in *An Glór* and *Combar*. She married the poet and psychoanalyst Rupert Strong in 1943 and, nine children later, she entered Trinity College, in 1969, as a mature student. She worked in publishing, freelance journalism, teaching and as a facilitator in creative writing courses. Widely published and anthologised in Ireland and overseas, she frequently gave readings at home and abroad. Her poetry was translated into French, Italian and German. A frequent broadcaster in Irish and English, she was granted many travel bursaries and was a member of Aosdána. She published a collection of short stories, *Patterns* (Poolbeg Press, 1991) and two novels. She praised and delighted in the upsurge of women poets in contemporary Ireland and was supportive of young and emerging writers. Her poetry is characterised by generosity of spirit and is a true example of a long life lived to the full. Explored with considerable detachment, her themes are life, death, youth and age, each expressed in the highly achieved style which marks her as a major figure in Irish contemporary poetry. She continued in the eighth decade of her life to write poetry and prose in Irish and in English. Her death, in August 1999, left literary Ireland feeling a profound sense of loss.

POETRY COLLECTIONS

In Irish
Cirt Oibre. (1980). Baile Átha Cliath, Coiscéim.
Fuil agus Fallaí. (1983). Baile Átha Cliath, Coiscéim.
Aoife faoi Ghlas. (1990). Baile Átha Cliath, Coiscéim.
An Sagart Pinc. (1990). Baile Átha Cliath, Coiscéim.
Nobel. (1998). Baile Átha Cliath, Coiscéim.

In English
Poetry Quartos. (1943-45). Dublin, Runa Press
Songs of Living. (1961). Dublin, Runa Press.
Sarah, in Passing. (1974). Dublin, Dolmen Press.
Flesh – The Greatest Sin. (1980). Runa Press, Dublin. Reprinted
    Attic Press, Dublin (1993).
My Darling Neighbour. (1985). Beaver Row Press, Dublin.
Let Live. (1990). Salmon Publishing, Galway.
Spatial Nosing. New and Selected Poems. (1993). Salmon
    Publishing, Galway.

HELLO

In the end you are quite alone,
you have really always been alone,
a queer odd one, *duine corr.*

Not in categorical slots
could you be gauged,
always wishing immeasurables.

Not fitting in,
you cannot be measured,
are not comparable

with the other old who, valiant,
ride bicycles at eighty, walk
weighty dogs, negotiate traffic.

You cannot even set up the ironing board
– your shoulders lock – nor
unscrew the safety tops of daily jars.

There is help, of course, but
you fear to be a nuisance,
request any aid. Face it,
to be old is to be innately loath
to invite rejection, to dread yourself
prattling, inept attempt towards inclusion,

and yet not to give a damn:
let happen – it will happen anyhow
as has happened all your years.

You have mostly attempted your best.
It was poor stuff, often. You wished
it better, always better, but learned

something of mercy towards the blemished
thing you are. It will all subsume along
with all you ever loved: those you've borne,

mountains at evening, meadows in the morning;
mix of tongues; along with the unachievable;
great ache outwards; yearning unaccountable.

You will recognize the final solitariness,
hold hands out to it:
the lone rock, empty bone.

It will all subsume and, finally, you
will be part of that 'It', the great Nothing,
the total thing: Hello!

Ronda, Andalucia, June 1998.

Breda Sullivan

(1945-)

Poet and teacher. Trained as a primary teacher, she taught in Streete on the Longford/Westmeath border. She wrote short stories until marriage and child-raising interrupted her writing. In 1987 she joined the Granard Writers' Group. She won first prize in the Gerard Manley Hopkins Poetry Competition in 1990 and 1992 and a collection of her poetry was chosen for the anthology *Six For Gold* published by *The Works* in Wexford (1990) Her poetry has appeared in many magazines, and periodicals, including *The Salmon* and *Writing in the West*, and she has been a prizewinner in poetry competitions in Ireland including the National Women's Poetry Competition. Her collections contain poems of memory, desire, fear and hope, written in a concise, powerfully simple, style.

POETRY COLLECTIONS

A Smell of Camphor. (1992). Galway, Salmon Publishing.
After the Ball. (1998). County Clare, Salmon Publishing.

WHAT I REMEMBER ....

is a baby
lying crosswise
on the bed

my aunt's face
damp
when I kissed her

a hackney cab
my uncle in the back
the white box on his lap

the midwife burying
baby clothes
in earth and ashes.

When she was gone
my mother dug them up
rinsed them in the sink

hung them on the line
saying waste
was a sin

and please God
they would be needed
again.

Alice Taylor

(1938-)

Poet and novelist. Born in County Cork and lives in Inishannon. Her three memoirs were enthusiastically received; the first, *To School Through the Fields* (1988) sold 175,000 copies in its first year of publication. Her two collections of poetry are marked with her descriptions of country life and people, written with the same feeling and charm she brought to prose descriptions of her childhood.

POETRY COLLECTIONS

Close to the Earth. (1989). County Kerry, Brandon Books.
Going to the Well. (1998). County Kerry, Mount Eagle Publications.

BATTERED CHALICE

God's day,
The birds and sun
Celebrate his creation.
You pick the daisies
With such joy in your hands;
Little child in the body of a man,
You are the host
In a battered chalice.
"Daoine le Dia," old people said,
And how wise they were
Because you live within
The circle of God's arm;
Not for you
The snares of this world,
You walk above man's narrow vision.

Kate Thompson

(1956-)

 Poet and fiction writer. Born in Yorkshire, she now lives in Galway. She worked with racehorses in England and the USA. Studied Law at Central London Polytechnic and later did diverse voluntary work in India. Attended Santiniketan (Rabindranath Tagore's University) as an extra-mural student and studied Gandhi's life and philosophy. Having stayed in an ashram, she learned yoga and qualified as a teacher. She came to Ireland, settled in County Clare and was a member of the North Clare Writers' Workshop. Her poetry and fiction has been published in several anthologies of new writing in Ireland and in literary magazines. She writes novels for children and adults, which have been published by the Bodley Head (1997, 1998) and Virago (1997). Her poems reflect her extraordinary life and vision.

POETRY COLLECTION

There is Something. (1992). Galway, Salmon Publishing / Washington USA, The Signpost Press Inc.

STONES

This mountain-top pierces the sky.
I scale its steep sides
And perch on its head
Like a wind-ruffled bird.
Clouds drift, above and below.

"As old as the hills"
The old people say.
This mountain, then,
Marks the beginning of time,
The last outpost of outreaching mind.

But like a rejoinder
Rain touches my hair,
Runs down the rocks,
Begins its return to the sea.
It brightens some stones,
Smooth as skin,
Round as plums,
Beach shingle
Where no beach could be.

And time becomes myth.
These pebbles were turned
In the mill of some tide
That no mussel awaited;
An ocean
No tongue ever tasted.

I stand like a myth-ruffled bird
In the great mill of time
And the rain runs down rocks
And the plum pebbles prove
That, whatever they say,
There is nothing so old
– Not even the hills –
There is nothing so old
As the sea.

Judith Thurley
(1958-)

Poet and nurse. Born in Bangor, County Down where she still lives. She was educated at the New University of Ulster (Coleraine) where she received a BA in Spanish and French. Later she lived and taught English in Madrid, graduating from the Universidad Complutense in 1981. She qualified as a registered General Nurse from Belfast City Hospital in 1987. A member of Ards Writers Group, County Down, led by poets Janet Shepperson and Martin Mooney, her poetry appeared in the *Belfast Newsletter*, *Newtownards Chronicle*, and *Write On*. She has read at numerous festivals including the Belfast Festival at Queen's University and participated in the award-winning ITV programme "Festival Virgin".

POETRY COLLECTION *

Listening for Hedgehogs. (1995). Belfast, Lapwing Publications.

I AM THE WOMAN

for Joan Newmann

i am the woman who shows her girls
the purple borage turn pink in the barley water;
i am the mother who makes the Ulster fry
when all around are eating tacos;
i am the woman who lifts her skirt
and dances steps to the corner,
who knows all the words to all the songs
and sings her daughters into sleep.

i am the woman who cuts the turf
who climbs the hill and digs the earth
to plant the tree that shades the woman
who bears the child.
i am she who bleeds with the moon,
delivers the child and cleanses the wound;
i lay out the dead.

i am the woman who flies the plane
who trims the jib and drives the train,
who skippers the winning boat round Ireland.
i am she who burns the sweet grass braid,
who fills her home with a light so pure
no darkness reaches the door.
i carry the Gartan clay.

already i am history.
let the children say, laughing
when they are grown:
do you remember ould Ma Thurley
with the frizzy hair and the freckles?
she was the woman who broke the spade
her daughters gave her
over the head of the man who betrayed her.
you should have seen the blood.

Áine Uí Fhoghlú

(1959-)

Poet, teacher and folklorist. Born in London, she lived in Australia until 1963, when her family moved home to Ireland. She lives in the Ring Gaeltacht, an Irish speaking area of County Waterford. She was educated locally and received her BA degree from University College, Cork. A contributor to the book *The Ballads and Songs of Waterford from 1487*, by Dermot Power, she also completed a literary standardization of *Scéalta Mhicil* (1923), republished by Coláiste na Rinne in 1997. A broadcast journalist with Raidio na Gaeltachta, she has compiled a collection of folklore from her area on video tape which she hopes to publish in book form. Her poetry won First Prize in the Dun Laoghaire/Rathdown Libraries International Poetry Competition in 1997 and she has written two plays, *Baile na hAinnise* and *An Deontas,* which were performed in County Waterford.

POETRY COLLECTION

Aistear Aonair. (1999). Baile Átha Cliath, Coiscéim.

REILIG AN TSLÉIBHE

Tá na hiomairí sléibhe tréigthe fadó
        Is na toibreacha imithe i ndísc
Tá an fothrach fuar ina sheasamh –
        Ar éigean
Is scaipeadh na gcarraig 's na gcloch
Mar an scaipeadh a tháinig anallód
Ar arm na mbocht.

Ach cé go machnaímid orthu, anois is arís,
        Beag ár gciall
Ar uafás na linne is orthu
        Siúd a d'fhulaing an ciapadh.
Ár gcompoirdí daonna, 'siad san ár ndéithe
I saol seo an mhorgáiste is
        Sladmhargaí na húrbhliana.

Ní cluichí ríomhairí ba chúram
        Don cholainn bheag feoite úd
Ach impí go réidhfí
        Faobhar an ocrais agus pianta páis'
Ní fheicfí páipéirí milseán
        Ná bosca bruscair lán
Ag lucht na gcnámh lom 's na gcreatlach fáin
Ar thaobh an tsléibhe a bhí á thréigint
        Ag arm na mbocht.

Ach airímse do scread ar an ngaoith
Nuair a shiúlann an Poncánach bolgach
Lena spéaclaí dorcha
Ar do chroí.

THE MOUNTAIN GRAVEYARD

The mountainside furrows are long since deserted
And the spring-wells all gone dry
The cold grey ruins just barely standing
And the scattered boulders and stones
Like the scattering hordes of old,
The legions of poor.

But though we ponder on their plight
– just now and then –
Little sense can we make
Of the horror of their night
Or of those who suffered the torment.

Our human comforts have become our Gods
In our world of mortgages
And new-year sales.
Computer games were not the cares
Of withered frames beseeching relief
From hunger pangs and torturous pains.

No empty sweetpapers nor waste from the tables
Of the bare-boned
And wayward skeletons
On the rugged mountain
Being daily deserted
By the army of poor.

But I hear your cries on the wind
When the bloated and dark glassed tourist
Who never knew you
Tramples on your soul.

trans. author. (*The author does not consider this
English version a poem in itself but rather as a key to
understanding the original*).

252

Máire Uí Nuanáin

(1929-)

Poet and teacher. Born on Inis Mór, the largest of the Aran Islands, County Galway. She was educated at the Dominican Convent, Eccles Street, Dublin and at University College, Galway where she received her BA degree in Celtic Studies. She later taught Latin and various other subjects in Kylemore Abbey, Connemara, Mount Anville, Dublin and in St. John's, Tralee. Her poems have been published in *Samhlaíocht Aniar*, *Aistir* and *Feasta*. She is a regular contributor to a Writers' Workshop in Tralee. Like the great Aran poet Máirtín Ó Direáin, her poetry is filled with the richness of her birthplace, and all that this unique heritage brings with it.

POETRY COLLECTION

Tuirne Mháire. (1998). Baile Átha Cliath, Coiscéim.

NÁ CAOIN

Scríobh dán grinn adúirt tú
le muid a chur ag gáire
ach ní féidir leis an ngáire a theacht
go mbíonn an brón ligthe.

Trí gáir ar cnoc
a lig clann Tuireann,
trí gáir ar cnoc
leis an mbrón a ligean.

Lig dom mar sin mo bhrón a ligean
agus nuair a bheas mo chroí ar nós an linbh
inseod duit dán
a chuirfeas ionat dinglis.

LET GO YOUR GRIEF

"Write a happy poem," you said,
"To make us laugh,"
But laughter cannot come
Until sorrow has been expressed.

From a high hill
Clann Tuireann of old
Gave three wild cries
To express their sorrow.

Let me now express my sorrow
And when my heart is young again
I'll write you a poem
Guaranteed to tickle.

trans. author.

255

Jean Valentine
(1934)

Poet and teacher. Born in Chicago, she graduated from Radcliffe College in 1956. She has been the recipient of a Guggenheim Fellowship and awards from the National Endowment for the Arts, the New York State Council for the Arts, the Bunting Institute and from the Rockefeller Foundation. She has lived most of her life in New York City where she teaches at Sarah Lawrence College. She lived in County Sligo from 1989 to 1996 and has been a regular contributor to many Irish literary journals and reviews. She was a popular workshop leader throughout Ireland and spent time at The Tyrone Guthrie Centre at Annaghmakerrig. Among the American prizes she has won for her poetry are the Yale Younger Poets' Award, the Maurice English Prize and the Sara Teasdale Award. She received two Artsflight awards from the Irish Arts Council in 1993 and 1994. Her return to live in New York has left the Irish poetry community, in particular Irish women poets, without her warm generosity. Her distinctive poetic contribution is an important part of the canon of twentieth-century Irish poetry written by women.

POETRY COLLECTIONS

Dream Barker and Other Poems. (1965). New Haven, Yale
    University Press.
Pilgrims. (1969). New York, Farrar, Straus and Giroux.
Ordinary Things. (1974). New York, Farrar, Straus and Giroux.
The Messenger. (1979). New York, Farrar, Straus and Giroux.
Home Deep Blue. (1988). Cambridge, Alice James Books.
The River at Wolf. (1992). Cambridge, Alice James Books.
The Under Voice – Selected Poems. (1995). Galway, Salmon Publishing.
Growing Darkness, Growing Light. (1997). Pittsburgh, Carnegie
    Mellon Press.

LITTLE MAP

The white pine

the deer coming closer

the ant
in my bowl
-- where did she go
when I brushed her out?

The candle
-- where does it go?

Our brush with each other
-- two animal souls
without cave
image
or
word

Noelle Vial

(1959-)

Poet. Born in Killybegs, County Donegal where she was educated. Co-founded the Killybegs' Writers Group in 1982. She has worked as the creative writing instructor at the local Vocational School. In November 1994 she won the Hennessy Literary Award for best poetry by an emerging writer and has been published in many Irish literary magazines. In April 1996, she toured in the USA during National Poetry Month. She has been a creative writing instructor for the Pushkin Prizes trust and was the Southern facilitator of *Writing across Borders*, a project which was EU-funded for peace and reconciliation. Together with organising poetry festivals, workshops and readings in association with Donegal County Library and Arts Centre, she has been a literary advisor to the Errigal Arts Festival. An adjudicator of The William Allingham Poetry Award, she has been an award-winner in a large number of poetry competitions including the Patrick MacGill Summer School Award for Poetry in 1983 and in 1994. A participant in the National Writers' Workshop in 1983, she also spent time at the Tyrone Guthrie Centre at Annaghmakerrig. Her poetry is underlined by a raw and genuine honesty and her approach is irreverent and independent.

POETRY COLLECTION

Promiscuous Winds. (1995). Oregon, USA, Story Line Press.

CHIEF MOURNER

At the foot of Conarade
a grieving man is burning
his wife's belongings.

The mountain is snow tipped:
he is cut off from the townland;
the passing condolences,
the well-meaning handshake
'Sorry for your trouble.'

Part of him is gone –
his stare is vacant.
No-one has the courage
to meet his eyes,
no-one has the courage to call.

In the village below,
townspeople watch
the black smoke turn
to a red dancing flame –

escaping from behind
a private screen of firs.

Oonagh Warke

(1957-)

Poet and reviewer. Born in County Derry and educated at Queen's University, Belfast and University College, Dublin. She graduated with a BA in English Literature and Language and an MA in Anglo-Irish Studies. She worked as a researcher in the University of Ulster at Jordanstown, moved to Brussels in 1986 and later to Dublin. After a series of temporary research posts she developed an interest in working with original documents and in 1989 she returned to full-time study, qualifying as an archivist in 1990. She then worked for the National Archives for three years, almost exclusively on the Irish Land Commission and Church Temporalities Commission archives, before moving to the Public Record Office of Northern Ireland in 1993. In 1996 she transferred to the mainstream Civil Service, working initially on environmental legislation and latterly on community development. Currently living on the north coast of County Derry, she has resumed the classes in Irish which she began in Dublin, and reviews occasionally for *Books Ireland* on poetry and other aspects of cultural history. Some of the poems in her pamphlet *Blood Ties* have previously been published in the New Irish Writing page of *The Irish Press*, *Chapman* and in *Poetry Ireland Review*.

POETRY COLLECTION *

Blood Ties. (1998). Belfast, Lapwing Publications.

LEARNING IRISH

Is a stranger knocking at my door
Who might or might not turn out
To be my grandfather, familiar only
From photographs, anecdotes, my father
Drumming his fingers on the edge
Of any table, and yet not then
A total stranger but strangely kin.
I shyly try on his coat and hat,
Take up his cane, and find myself
Walking in his footsteps, out into
The crisp November day ("Go out
The door you came in, daughter")
And down the lane ("If it
Were any shorter it wouldn't be
Long enough") to the farmhouse,
The wind soughing in the hawthorn
An elusive vowel teasing the consonants
Of my new vocabulary, the red berries
Ready to be picked ("If the coat fits,
Wear it"). His moustache twiches
As I wind my shoulders into the tweed
(will my brothers call me Joseph?)
And he raises the latch on the half-door,
Stepping jauntily before me across
The ray of sunshine striking the shelf
Of empty jamjars by the fire.
I hang the coat carefully over a chair,
Roll up sleeves and put the kettle on
While he whistles an air I'm almost sure
I've heard my father play before.

Sabine Wichert

(1942-)

 Poet and teacher. Born in Graudenz, West Prussia (now Grudziadz, Poland) she grew up and was educated in West Germany. She has been teaching history at Queen's University, Belfast since 1971 and has a special interest in the visual arts. She was a member of the Arts Council of Northern Ireland from the mid-1980s to 1994 and is a member of the Board of Annaghmakerrig appointed by both Arts Councils in Ireland. Her publications include *Miranda*, a pamphlet from Lapwing, Belfast. Published extensively in journals over a number of years, including *The Salmon* magazine's earliest editions. Her poetry links her adopted town of Belfast with her European experience. It spans a lifetime of family, friends and upbringing.

POETRY COLLECTIONS

Tin Drum Country. (1995). Galway, Salmon Publishing.
Sharing Darwin. (1999). County Clare, Salmon Publishing.

EASTER AT AILESBURY GROVE

for Ailbhe

The train that brought me here
searched for escapes in rivers,
trees and travel, childish memories
on literary pages under whitish sky.

This courtyard lets the child
play in the sun and concentrates
the presence on Lydia:
this is bearable, the protected light
tempts me to settle with myself.

Enda Wyley

(1966-)

Poet and teacher. Born in Dublin, she graduated from Carysfort Teacher Training College with first place in English Literature. She teaches in Dublin's inner city. In 1992 she received an MA in Creative Writing from Lancaster University. A participant in workshops with Paul Durcan, Michael Longley and Paula Meehan, her poems have appeared in publications in Ireland and abroad. An award winner in the 1992 British National Poetry Competition, she has read her poetry on RTÉ Radio 1, Sydney University Radio and for Poetry Ireland/Abbey Theatre International Women's Day, 1993. She received an Arts Council Bursary for Literature in 1997, and in 1998 she read her poetry at literary festivals including The Maastricht International Poetry Festival. Her collections include love poems and poems of anger and hope, written in a style suggestive of the influences of Russian, Greek and Irish poets, in particular Akhmatova, Auden, Cavafy and Kavanagh.

POETRY COLLECTIONS

Eating Baby Jesus. (1993). Dublin, The Dedalus Press.
Socrates in the Garden. (1998). Dublin, The Dedalus Press.

WEDDING GIFT

i. m. Raymond Carver, 1938-1988

Salmon leaping eternally, against a well-lit sky,
bend ecstatic towards the waterfall, in the wedding gift you painted.
Like Chekhov, I map new routes from the town where I'll soon die

but now and then I stop, admiring these fish that try
to tussle free from the river; a push, then they've succeeded –
salmon leaping eternally, against a well-lit sky.

If I'd even a year! I make a list: eggs, hot choc, buy
cigarettes labelled "Now", at last book that Antarctica ticket!
Like Chekhov, I map new routes from the town where I'll soon die

and must continue the struggle upstream, despite the lie
I lived: once drunk, wife-leaver, bum – but now, like determined
salmon, leaping eternally against a well-lit sky

in this picture you gave us for our last fling; that high,
sad, tacky affair in a Reno chapel, after the blood I'd coughed.
Like Chekhov, I map new routes from the town where I'll soon die

and am travelling faster now, suddenly floating high
where my poems make me beloved; yet still, I watch over my head
salmon leaping eternally, against a well-lit sky –
like Chekhov, I map new routes from the town where I'll soon die.

Ann Zell

(1933-)

Poet. Born in Idaho, USA. She lived in New York and London before settling in West Belfast in 1980. She began to write poetry when working as a medical secretary in the Royal Victoria Hospital, Belfast. A member of the Word of Mouth poetry collective, her work has appeared in many publications including *Virago New Poets*, *The Atlanta Review*, *Word of Mouth* (Blackstaff Press, Belfast, 1996), *Poetry Ireland Review* and *Verse*. Her voice is one of the strongest to appear in contemporary women's poetry from Northern Ireland in recent years.

POETRY COLLECTION

Weathering. (1998). County Clare, Salmon Publishing.

UNTITLED

My aunt's letter, with poems
 her sister wrote at 17
  came after a weekend spent
   discussing poetry and foremothers.
And I never knew my mother wrote.

Close mountains oppress me.
 Mountains were her city's walls
  murals for all her weather
   shifting colours and dimensions
with the angle and intensity of light.

If she wrote in our crowded
 house on the edge of desert
  where nothing but sunsets
   held the eye - no near mountains
to shield her eyes from too much distance

she must have done it at midnight
 and burned the evidence.
  There were only dustballs under
   the bed where we played hide-and-seek.
No poems were found among her things.

I know some of the reasons why
 women stop writing.   She may
  have had others.   She may have been
   lonely in the company of children, or
the children may have been her poems

and what are poems anyway?
 Poised on the threshold-of-womanhood
  she wrote about Sappho and the moon
   and mountains, and stepped into a room
prepared for her. My mother never wrote.

Afterword

The original research for *The White Page/An Bhileog Bhán Twentieth-Century Irish Women Poets* was submitted as a dissertation for the MA Degree in Women's Studies, in the Faculty of Arts at University College, Dublin in August 1997. Ailbhe Smyth, Director of the Women's Education, Research and Resource Centre, who was my supervisor, first suggested that I consider book publication. I wish to thank her for this advice and for her help and guidance throughout.

In February 1999, together with my publisher, Jessie Lendennie of Salmon Publishing Limited, County Clare, the decision was made to develop the study and to publish it in book form. I wrote to more than one hundred poets, with an invitation to contribute one poem of their choice, published or unpublished, accompanied by a photograph of themselves. In the case of poets deceased, letters were sent to their families and publishers. The immediate response was both generous and enthusiastic.

In editing this book I have not attempted to include a literary or historical context for the period I am dealing with, other than of a cursory nature. Neither have I attempted any critical analysis of the poetry, including instead, in most cases, a short personal response to each poet's work. My index of authors does not claim to be fully authoritative. Included are poets who have published at least one collection of poetry and, in some instances, poetry published in pamphlet form.

Particular attention has been paid to listing birth years and places, and education. Relationships to writing groups have been noted where relevant. Acknowledgments of Arts Council bursaries, literary awards, prizes and travel grants have also been included, together with information on individual poets writing in genres other than poetry.

The work is arranged alphabetically by the poets' surnames and chronologically by multi-volume poets. With few exceptions volumes published by individual poets born before 1920 have not been listed. Libraries and bookshops, including second-hand bookshops, were used extensively as I researched this book. Many titles were found to be out of print so it became essential that personal contact be made with individual poets whose work fell into this category. Contact with many poets no longer publishing and those who do not live now in Ireland created difficulties. I received generous help from the many people I made contact with during the course of writing this book. I compiled, as a result, a large file of letters and personal responses which addressed themselves not only to me and my research, but to Ireland and to Irish poetry. Permission for me to use biographical details was not in any single case denied.

I am especially grateful for the support and advice received throughout my time at UCD from my fellow students and friends and from my tutors and lecturers. Theo Dorgan, Director of Poetry Ireland, Niall MacMonagle and Gabriel Fitzmaurice deserve a special thanks for the generous sharing of libraries and their interest in both the original research and in this book. I am grateful to the Irish women poets included who supported and corresponded with me, telephoned and gave me gifts of their collections of poetry. I am grateful for their voices and above all I wish to acknowledge their courage in sustaining the life of writing as women in this culture. Anne Ward became the angel in my house, patiently typing, filing and generally keeping order on a project that often threatened to overwhelm me. My friend and fellow poet Anne Kennedy died of cancer on September 29th, 1998. I was conscious of the fact that she and I had so often discussed the possibility of this book coming into being and how much she would have valued it. Her spirit guided me throughout and it is with both the sorrow of her loss and the joy of remembering her that I dedicate this book to her memory.

I thank Jessie Lendennie and Siobhán Hutson for their patient responses to my many calls and queries and for the help I received from Salmon Publishing. David Burke, editor of *The Tuam Herald*, deserves a word of thanks. Jim Carney's friendship, support and invaluable help with reading and re-reading the text and with proof-reading is gratefully acknowledged.

Several people gave me information, support, ideas, time, encouragement and books. I am especially grateful to Pádraig Ó Snodaigh, Catríona Clutterbuck, Lia Mills, Kathleen Cain, Anne Ulry Colman, Janice Fitzpatrick-Simmons, Eamon Grennan, Clare Barrington, Gráinne Blair, Monica Heneghan, Dr. Anthony Sharpe, Colin Smythe, Professor Robert Welch, Brian McBreen, Peter Fallon, Seamus Hosey, Dr. Riana O'Dwyer, John F. Deane, Dennis Greig, Joanne Mulroe, Joan Long, Mark Patrick Hederman and Eilish Hogge.

Acknowledgement is made to all the publishers and poets who gave permission to reprint photographs in this book. Fees for reprinting of poems and photographs were waived in all cases in view of royalties from sales of this book being donated to the Leukaemia Trust at University College Hospital, Galway. I thank the Bank of Ireland (Tuam Branch) for their help with achieving part sponsorship for the publication of this book. I thank the poet Colette Nic Aodha who kindly agreed to help with the editing of the biographical and bibliographical notes on the contributors to this book who write in Irish. Thanks also to the artist Gwen O'Dowd for generously giving permission for her fine painting to be used on the cover of this book and on the flier/order form. Thanks to Cathal Ó

Luain who generously gave permission for the late Caitlín Maude's poem title, *An Bhileog Bhán*, to be used as part of the title of this book and also for allowing the text of her poem to be printed, along with its translation, on the book cover.

Finally, a debt of thanks to my husband Joe McBreen and my children who believed in me and in the importance of this task to Irish poetry.

Joan McBreen

Acknowledgements

Grateful acknowledgement is made to the poets and their publishers for poems included in this book. *Some poems are published here for the first time. **Others have appeared in magazines and journals but are not found in collections to date.

Nuala Archer. "The Lost Glove Is Happy," *The Hour of Pan / amá*. (Salmon, 1992).

Leland Bardwell. "Two Lessons in Anatomy: York Street, Dublin," *The White Beach, New and Selected Poems 1960-1998*. (Salmon, 1998).

* Sara Berkeley. "Emergence."

Jean Bleakney. "A Woman Of Our Times," *The Ripple Tank Experiment*. (Lagan, 1999).

Eavan Boland. "The Blossom," *The Lost Land*. (Carcanet, 1998).

* Rosita Boland. "Diamonds."

* Eva Bourke. "The Nightsinger."

** Máire Bradshaw. "eurydice."

* Deirdre Brennan. "Ceilteanas."

Lucy Brennan. "The Wedding Dress," *Migrants All* (watershedBooks, 1999).

Heather Brett. "Bloodthirst," *The Touch-Maker*. (Alternative Publishing / Literary Publishing, 1994).

* Patricia Burke-Brogan. "Patterns."

Catherine Byron. "Minding You," *The Getting of Vellum*. (Salmon / Blackwater, 1999).

Louise C. Callaghan. "The Palatine Daughter Marries a Catholic," *The Puzzle-Heart*. (Salmon, 1999).

* Siobhán Campbell. "The Halting."

Rosemary Canavan. "Sea Widow," *The Island*. (Story Line, 1994).

Moya Cannon. From "Introductions," *The Parchment Boat*. (Gallery, 1997).

Moya Cannon. "Night," *The Parchment Boat*. (Gallery, 1997).

Ruth Carr. "We Share the Same Skin," *There is a House.*
(Summer Palace, 1999).

Juanita Casey. "Zen and Now," *Eternity Smith and other poems.*
(Dolmen, 1985).

Glenda Cimino. "What the Court Clerk said," *Cicada.* (Beaver
Row, 1987).

** Anne Cluysenaar. "A Presence."

Susan Connolly. "For The Stranger," *For The Stranger.*
(Dedalus, 1993).

Roz Cowman. "Dream of the Red Chamber," *The Goose Herd.*
(Salmon, 1999).

Vicki Crowley. "The New Canvas." *Oasis in a Sea of Dust.*
(Salmon, 1992).

Yvonne Cullen. "For While We'll Write Letters, And For When
We Won't," *Invitation To The Air.* (iTaLiCs Press, 1998).

Paula Cunningham. "Sometimes dancing," *A Dog called chance.*
(Smith / Doorstop Books, 1999).

* Bríd Dáibhís. "Leaca."

** Moyra Donaldson. "I Do Not."

* Katie Donovan. "Him."

* Mary Dorcey. "Each Day our First Night."

Anna-Marie Dowdican. "Mine Be," *Imagine.* (Black Battler, 1998).

Katherine Duffy. "Weatherwitch," *The Erratic Behaviour of Tides.*
(Dedalus, 1998).

Martina Evans. "A Quiet Man," *All Alcoholics Are Charmers*
(Anvil, 1998).

Maurice Farley. "A House By Lough Carra," *Before the Cattle
Raid and Other Poems.* (Lapwing, 1998).

* Pauline Fayne. "Optimism."

Janice Fitzpatrick-Simmons. "Ballroom Dancing," *Starting at Purgatory.*
(Salmon, 1999).

Anne-Marie Fyfe. "Hallstand."

Isobel Gamble. "Like Mercator," *The Orchard.* (Lapwing, 1998).

Sarah Gatley. "Wild Affair," *Black Line On White.* (Lapwing, 1997).

Catherine Graham. "The Watch," *The Watch.* (Abbey, 1998).

Angela Greene. "Letting Go," *Silence and the Blue Night.*
(Salmon, 1993).

Pamela Greene. "voice in a bell jar," *Heartland.* (Lapwing, 1998).

Rene Greig. "Filigree Network," *Through a Hedge Backwards.*
(Ha'penny, 1999).

Vona Groarke. "House-bound," *Other People's Houses.*
(Gallery, 1999).

* Kerry Hardie. "She Replies To Carmel's Letter."

Tess Hurson. "In The Snowstorm," *Vivarium.* (Lagan, 1997).

* Anne Le Marquand Hartigan. "Epistles in Winter."

Anne Haverty. "Ladies Waiting Room, Thurles Station,"
The Beauty of the Moon. (Chatto & Windus, 1999).

* Rita Ann Higgins. "The Weather Beaters."

* Máire Holmes. "Iarfhlaith."

Biddy Jenkinson. "Maidir leis na Dánta sa Leabhar seo," *Uiscí Beatha.*
(Coiscéim, 1988).

* Maeve Kelly. "Primo Levi's Prayer."

Rita Kelly. "Fare Well – Beir Beannacht," *Fare Well, Beir Beannacht –
Poems in English and Irish.* (Attic, 1990).

Anne Kennedy. "With One Continuous Breath," *The Dog Kubla
Dreams My Life.* (Salmon, 1994).

** Jessie Lendennie. "Between Us."

Catherine Phil MacCarthy. "Sand Goddess," *The Blue Globe.*
(Blackstaff, 1998).

Carmen Mac Garrigle. "Adamant," *Journey From The Dead Room.*
(Lapwing, 1998).

Eilish Martin. "Days of Abstinence," *slitting the tongues of jackdaws.*
(Summer Palace, 1999).

Orla Martin. "Aunts Mattered," *The Trek from Venus.*
(bradshaw books, 1996).

Caitlín Maude. "Liobar," *Caitlín Maude, file, poet, poeta* (edizioni dal
sud), (Italy, 1985) and *Caitlín Maude, Dánta.* (Coscéim, 1984).

Joan McBreen. "The Mountain Ash," *A Walled Garden in Moylough*
(Salmon and Story Line, 1995).

* Kathleen McCracken. "Green Pool With Lightning."

* Linda McDermott. "The River."

* Medbh McGuckian. "The Presence Of Her Absence."

* Ethna McKiernan. "Driving The Coast Road To Dingle."

Kathleen McPhilemy. "Christmas 1989," *A Tented Peace.*
(Katabasis, 1995).

* Liz McSkeane. "Cold Turkey."

Máighréad Medbh. "My Day," *Tenant.* (Salmon,1999).

* Paula Meehan. "The Trapped Woman of the Internet."

Máire Mhac an tSaoi. "Shoa," *Shoa agus Dánta Eile*. (forthcoming).

Áine Miller. "The Silence Cloth," *Goldfish in a Baby Bath*. (Salmon, 1994).

Lynda Moran. "Famine Song," *The Truth about Lucy*. (Beaver Row, 1985).

* Sinéad Morrissey. "On Waitakere Dam."

Iris Murdoch. "Motorist and Dead Bird," *The Music of What Happens*. (BBC, 1981).

Lizz Murphy. "Cold Enough For Snow," *Pearls and Bullets*. (Island Press, Australia, 1997).

* Joan Newmann. "Remembering Bridget Cleary."

* Colette Nic Aodha. "Barr Taoide," *Baill Seirce*. (Coiscéim, 1999).

Máire Áine Nic Gearailt. "Teicheadh," *Ó Ceileadh an Bhreasáil*. (Coiscéim, 1992).

Eiléan Ní Chuilleanáin. "Studying The Language," *The Brazen Serpent*. (Gallery, 1994).

* Eiléan Ní Chuilleanáin. "Astray."

Nuala Ní Dhomhnaill. "Tusa," *Cead Aighnis*. (An Sagart, 1998).

Máirín Ní Dhomhnalláin. "Fear an Chlóca Léith," *Sin Mar a Bhí*. (Coiscéim, 1997).

Colette Ní Ghallchóir. "I nGairdín na u-Úll," *Idir Dhá Ghleann*. (Coiscéim, 1999).

Áine Ní Ghlinn. "Tú Féin is Mé Féin," *Deora Nár Caoineadh*. (Coiscéim and Dedalus, 1996).

* Brighid Ní Mhóráin. "An Cosán Bán."

* Jean O'Brien. "The Gates of Horn."

Julie O'Callaghan. "The Great Blasket Island," *What's What*. (Bloodaxe, 1991).

* Clairr O'Connor. "Outcast Elder."

Mary O'Donnell. "In the Tuileries," *Unlegendary Heroes*. (Salmon, 1998).

** Kathleen O'Driscoll. "War Child."

Sheila O'Hagan. "The Return of Odysseus to Ithaca," *The Troubled House*. (Salmon, 1995)

Nessa O'Mahoney. "Lament for a Shy Man," *Bar Talk*. (iTaLiCs, 1999).

* Mary O'Malley. "Fate."

Barbara Parkinson. "Leaving is the Price," *Any Change for the Jugglers*. (Salmon, 1995).

Evangeline Paterson. "Visitation," *A Game of Soldiers*. (Stride, 1997).

* Angela Patten. "At The Butcher's Shop."

Anne Peters. "The Green Martyrdom," *Rings of Green*.
(Colin Smythe Ltd., 1982).

** Rosemarie Rowley. "Fair-haired Donncha."

Deirdre Shanahan. "Land," *Legal Tender*. (Enitharmon, 1988).

** Janet Shepperson. "The Furthest North You Can Go."

Jo Slade. "From Where It Came," *Certain Octobers – Parfois en Octobre* (Editions Eireanna and Salmon 1997).

** Eithne Strong. "Hello."

Breda Sullivan. "What I Remember," *After the Ball*. (Salmon, 1998).

Alice Taylor. "Battered Chalice," *Close to the Earth*. (Brandon, 1989).

* Kate Thompson. "Stones."

Judith Thurley. "I am the Woman." *Listening For Hedgehogs*.
(Lapwing, 1995).

Áine Uí Fhoghlú. "Reilig an tSléibhe," Aistear Aonair.
(Cóiscéim 1999).

Máire Uí Nuanáin. "Ná Caoin," *Túirne Mháire*. (Coiscéim, 1998).

** Jean Valentine. "Little Map."

* Noelle Vial. "Chief Mourner."

Oonagh Warke. "The Piped Stream's Last Poem," *Blood Ties*.
(Lapwing, 1998).

Sabine Wichert. "Easter at Ailesbury Grove," *Tin Drum Country*.
(Salmon, 1995).

Enda Wyley. "Wedding Gift," *Eating Baby Jesus*. (Dedalus, 1994).

Ann Zell. "Untitled". *Weathering*. (Salmon, 1998).

The following sections of this book were part of the original M.A. research. They are included here as a guide and reference source for both general readers and students working in the field of contemporary Irish poetry.

General Biographical Reference Sources

Bourke, Eva. (1996). *With Green Ink: Contemporary Irish Poetry.* [Translated by Eva Bourke: Mit Grüner Tinte; Zeitgenossische Irische Lyrik.]. Germany, Bamberg.

Brady, Anne M. and Brian Cleeve. (eds.). (1985). *A Biographical Dictionary of Irish Writers.* Mullingar, Lilliput Press.

Buck, Claire. (ed.). (1992). *Bloomsbury Guide to Women's Literature.* London, Bloomsbury Publishing.

Colman, Anne Ulry. (1996). *A Dictionary of Nineteenth-Century Irish Women Poets.* Galway, Kenny's Bookshop Press.

Connerton Fallon, Ann. (1979). *Katharine Tynan.* Boston, Twayne.

Deane, Seamus. (gen. ed.). (1991). *The Field Day Anthology of Irish Writing.* 3 vols. Derry, Field Day Publications.

Donovan, Katie, A. Norman Jeffares and Brendan Kennelly. (1994). *Ireland's Women – Writings Past and Present.* Dublin, Gill and Macmillan.

Dorgan, Theo. (ed.). (1996). *Irish Poetry Since Kavanagh.* Dublin, Four Courts Press.

Haberstroh, Patricia Boyle. (1996). *Women Creating Women – Contemporary Irish Women Poets.* New York, Syracuse University Press / Dublin, Attic Press.

Hoff, Joan and Moureen Coulter (eds.). (1995). *Irish Women's Voices: Past and Present.* Bloomington Indiana, Indiana University Press.

Hogan, Robert. (editor-in-chief). (1996). *Dictionary of Irish Literature.* 2 vols. Revised and expanded edition. Westport, Connecticut, USA. Greenwood Press / London, Aldwych Press.

Kiberd, Declan. (1995). *Inventing Ireland – The Literature of the Modern Nation.* London, Jonathan Cape.

Kinsella, Thomas. (1995). *The Dual Tradition – An Essay on Poetry and Politics in Ireland*. Manchester, Carcanet Press. / Dublin, Peppercanister 18.

Ní Chuilleanáin, Eiléan. (ed.). (1985). *Irish Women: Image and Achievement*. Dublin, Arlen House Press.

Ní Dhuibhne, Eilís. (ed.). (1995). *Voices on the Wind – Women Poets of the Celtic Twilight*. Dublin, New Island Books.

Ormsby, Frank. (ed.). (1979). *Poets from the North of Ireland*. Belfast, The Blackstaff Press.

Ormsby, Frank. (ed.). (1992). *A Rage for Order – Poetry of The Northern Ireland Troubles*. Belfast, The Blackstaff Press.

Owen Weekes, Ann. (1993). *Unveiling Treasures: The Attic Guide To The Published Works of Irish Women Literary Writers*. Dublin, Attic Press.

Paterson, Evangeline. (1991). *What to do with your Poems*. Newcastle upon Tyne, Other Poetry Editions.

Welch, Robert (ed.). (1996). *The Oxford Companion to Irish Literature*. Oxford, Clarendon Press.

Anthologies Consulted

A partial list of anthologies cited and consulted:

Bolger, Dermot. (1986). *The Bright Wave – An Tonn Gheal: Poetry in Irish Now*. Dublin, Raven Arts Press.

Connolly, Susan and Catherine Phil MacCarthy. (1991). *How High The Moon – Boann & Other Poems* and *Sanctuary*. Dublin, Poetry Ireland / Co-operation North.

Crotty, Patrick. (ed.). (1995). *Modern Irish Poetry – an Anthology*. Belfast, Blackstaff Press.

Delanty, Greg and Nuala Ní Dhomhnaill. (eds.). (1995). *Jumping off Shadows: Selected Contemporary Irish Poets*. Cork, Cork University Press.

Dowson, Jane. (ed.). (1996). *Women's Poetry of the 1930s – A Critical Anthology*. London, Routledge.

Dunne, Sean. (ed.). (1985). *Poets of Munster – An Anthology*. London, Anvil Press / Dingle, County Kerry, Brandon Books.

Fallon, Peter and Derek Mahon. (eds.). (1990). *The Penguin Book of Contemporary Irish Poetry*. Middlesex, Penguin Books.

Fitzmaurice, Gabriel. (ed.). (1993). *Irish Poetry Now: Other Voices*. Dublin, Wolfhound Press.

Henry, P. L. (Selected and translated.). (1990). *Dánta Ban: Poems of Irish Women, early and modern*. Cork, The Mercier Press.

Hooley, Ruth. (1985). *The Female Line: Northern Irish Women Writers*. Belfast, Northern Ireland Women's Rights Movement.

Kelly, A. A. (ed.). (1987). *Pillars of the House: An Anthology of Verse by Irish Women from 1690 to the present*. Dublin, Wolfhound Press.

Kennelly, Brendan. (ed.). (1970). *The Penguin Book of Irish Verse*. Middlesex, Penguin Books.

Kiberd, Declan and Gabriel Fitzmaurice. (eds.). (1991). *An Crann Faoi Bhláth: The Flowering Tree*. Dublin, Wolfhound Press.

Kinsella, Thomas. (ed.). (1986). *The New Oxford Book of Irish Verse.*
Oxford, Oxford University Press.

MacDonagh, Donagh and Lennox Robinson. (eds.). (1958).
The Oxford Book of Irish Verse. Oxford, The Clarendon Press.

Montague, John. (ed.). (1974). *The Faber Book of Irish Verse.*
London, Faber and Faber.

O'Brien, Peggy. (ed.). (1999). *The Wake Forest Book of Irish Women's
Poetry 1967-2000.* Winston Salem N.C., Wake Forest University
Press.

Smyth, Ailbhe. (ed.). (1989). *Wildish Things: An Anthology of New
Irish Women's Writing.* Dublin, Attic Press.

Somerville – Arjat and Rebecca E. Wilson. (eds.). (1990). *Sleeping
with Monsters: Conversations with Scottish and Irish Women Poets.*
Dublin, Wolfhound Press.

Journals Consulted

Agee, Chris. (ed.). (1995). *Poetry: Contemporary Irish Poetry –*
A Special Double Issue. Chicago.

Archer, Nuala. (ed.). (1986). *The Midland Review: Contemporary Irish*
Women's Writing. Vol. 3 (Winter). Oklahoma, USA.

Boland, Eavan. (ed.). (1987). *The Women's Education Bureau,*
WEB Journal 1 (2), pp. 2-3. Dublin, Arlen House.

Boland, Eavan. (1993). *Seneca Review: New Voices in Irish Women's*
Poetry: An Introduction 23 (1+2). Geneva NY, Hobart and William
Smith Colleges.

Mac an tSaoi, Máire. (ed.). (1991). *Poetry Ireland Review* No. 31.
Dublin.

Olney, James and Dave Smith. (eds.). (1995). *The Southern Review –*
A Special Issue: Contemporary Irish Poetry and Criticism 31 (3).
Baton Rouge, LA, Louisiana State University Press.

Critical Studies Consulted

Allen-Randolph, Jody. (1991). Écriture Féminine and the Authorship of Self In Eavan Boland's *In Her Own Image. Colby Quarterly* 27 (1) pp. 48-59. Maine, Colby College Press.

Boland, Eavan. (1995). *Object Lessons – The Life of The Woman and The Poet in Our Time.* Manchester, Carcanet Press.

Denman, Peter. (1992). Rude Gestures? Contemporary Women's Poetry in Irish *Colby Quarterly* 28 (4), pp. 251-259. Maine. Colby College Press.

Donovan, Katie. (1988). *Irish Women Writers: Marginalised by Whom?* Dublin, Raven Arts Press.

Fogarty, Anne. (1995). Fault Lines, *Graph* 2 (1), pp. 18-25. Cork, Cork University Press.

Grennan, Eamon. (ed.). (1992). Contemporary Irish Poetry – Introduction. *Colby Quarterly* 28 (4), pp. 181-189. Maine, Colby College Press.

Ní Dhomhnaill, Nuala. (1992). What Foremothers? *Poetry Ireland Review* 36, pp. 18-31. Dublin, Poetry Ireland.

Tall, Deborah. (1988). Q and A with Eavan Boland *Irish Literary Supplement* 7 (2), pp. 39-40. Massachusetts, Boston College Press.

Index of Poets

Index of Poem Titles

Index of First Lines

Notes to the Text

The notes given here explain terms and references well known in Ireland but not perhaps to non-Irish readers.

Amharclann na Peacóige – The Peacock Theatre

Aosdána – This is an affiliation of artists engaged in literature, music and the visual arts. It was established by the Arts Council in 1981 to honour those artists whose work has made an outstanding contribution to the arts in Ireland, and to encourage and assist members in devoting their energies fully to their art.

Aran – Three dramatic islands off the coast of County Galway: *Inis Mór, Inis Meáin,* and *Inis Óirr* (Inishmore, Inishmaan and Inisheer). The poet Máirtín Ó Direáin came from Inis Mór.

Duais Bhord na Gaeilge – Prize awarded by *Bhord na Gaeilge.*

Duais Chuimhneacháin 1916 – Commemorative Prize marking the 1916 Easter Rising.

Oireachtas – *Oireachtas na Gaeilge* is an annual celebration of Irish culture, music and literature. *Duais an Oireachtais* is its major award for poetry.

Poetry Ireland / *Éigse Éireann* – This is an organisation supported by both Arts Councils of Ireland to promote and support poetry and poets in Ireland. It was founded in 1978 by poet and editor John F. Deane. Poetry Ireland organises readings nationally by poets from Ireland and abroad, publishes a bi-monthly newsletter and four issues annually of *Poetry Ireland Review.* Poets, scholars and the public are welcomed to the Austin Clarke Memorial Library comprising over 6,000 volumes. Together with organising the Writers-in-Schools Scheme which works extensively with international journals and literary festivals wishing to feature Irish poets. The Irish partner in the European translation network, Poetry Ireland has published books in translation by sixteen authors to date.

Raidio na Gaeltachta – The national broadcasting station for *Gaeltacht* (Irish-speaking) areas.

RTÉ – Raidio Telefís Éireann is the national broadcasting company in the Republic of Ireland.

sean-nós – Old style. Singing *as Gaeilge* (in Irish) in a traditional manner.

The Tyrone Guthrie Centre, Annaghmakerrig – Sir Tyrone Guthrie (1900-1971) was one of the foremost theatre directors of the 20th century. His sister, Mrs. Susan Butler, convinced her brother that he should leave the home of their mother, Norah Power, at Annaghmakerrig to Ireland as a "place of retreat for artists and such like creative creatures." Annaghmakerrig is administered by a Board appointed by the two Arts Councils of Ireland. It welcomes artists of all kinds and provenances to a unique working environment among the drumlins and lakes of County Monaghan in south Ulster.

The Great Book of Ireland – On June 11th 1989 the first two pages of this unique volume came into being with poems from poets Seamus Heaney and John Montague together with images by the artist Barrie Cooke. Made of vellum, it was the brainchild of Theo Dorgan, Director of Poetry Ireland, artist Gene Lambert and business manager Eamonn Martin. It includes poems inscribed by one hundred and forty-nine poets together with visual work from one hundred and twenty artists painted directly onto the pages. Nobel Prize winner Samuel Beckett's contribution was the last poem he ever wrote. Nine composers also wrote their music directly onto their individual pages. The book was presented and celebrated in the Royal Hospital, Kilmainham on the 25th of June 1991. It was a joint enterprise undertaken by the Clashganna Mills Trust, a charity for people with disabilities, and Poetry Ireland.

Editor's Notes

Jenkinson, Biddy – This is a pen name. This poet writes only in the Irish language and does not permit her poetry to be translated into English. In 'A Letter to the Editor' in the *Irish University Review* (Spring/Summer 1991, No. 34) she writes: "I prefer not to be translated into English in Ireland. It is a small rude gesture to those who think that everything can be harvested and stored without loss in an English speaking Ireland. If I were a corncrake I would feel no obligation to have my skin cured, my tarsi injected with formalin so that I could fill a museum shelf in a world that saw no need for my kind." Jenkinson's gift to *The White Page / An Bhileog Bhán* is her poem *as Gaeilge* (in Irish) together with her permission to use Mireille Harnett's French translation.

While every effort has been made to ensure that biographical and bibliographical details given in this work are accurate, it does not claim to be fully authoritative. The editor and publisher apologise to poets and their publishers for any errors or omissions in the acknowledgements and would be grateful to be notified of any corrections that should be incorporated in the next edition of this volume.